# THE
# GREAT BRITISH
# CHRISTMAS

Christmas dinner, 1850s.

# THE
# GREAT BRITISH
# CHRISTMAS

COMPILED BY
## MARIA HUBERT

SUTTON PUBLISHING

First published in the United Kingdom in 1999
Sutton Publishing Limited · Phoenix Mill · Thrupp
Stroud · Gloucestershire · GL5 2BU

British Library Cataloguing in Publication Data
A catalogue record for this book is available from the British Library.

ISBN 0-7509-2094-7

Typeset in 11/15½ Sabon.
Typesetting and origination by
Sutton Publishing Limited.
Printed in Great Britain by
Redwood, Trowbridge, Wiltshire.

# Contents

The Great British Christmas – An Introduction     1
*Maria Hubert*

Christmas Books     3
*William Makepeace Thackeray*

The Calennig     9

King Arthur's Christmas     10
*Sir Thomas Malory*

'Eddi's Service'     12
*Rudyard Kipling*

'The First Wassail'     14
*R. Acton*

A Horn of Mead     27
*Anon – A recipe for honeyed wine*

An Anglo-Norman Carol     28

The Second Shepherd's Play     31

A Hue and Cry After Christmas     33
*From a seventeenth-century broadsheet by*
*Simon Minc'd Pye*

'Old Christmas Still Comes!'     34

Christmas with the Diarists     38
*Samuel Pepys, John Evelyn and others*

Deck the Church with Evergreens     47
*From the* Spectator, *1712*

Love and Hot Cockles! 49
*From the* Spectator, *1711*

'Hallo Hogmanay!' 49
*D.B. Wyndham Lewis*

The Christmas Tree 55
*Charles Dickens*

Tales of the Christmas Cracker 68
*Maria Hubert and Michael Harrison*

The Twelfth Cake 75
*From* The Memoirs of a London Doll
*Richard Henry Horne*

The Royal Christmases of Queen Victoria 81

The Christmas Tree at Windsor Castle 93
*From the* Illustrated London News, *1848*

Mrs Beeton's Christmas Cake 95
*From* Mrs Beeton's Book of Household
Management, *1853*

'"Owed" to the Christmas Tree' 96
*'A Sharp Old File', 1853*

Christmas Eve at an Old Hertfordshire Farmhouse 101
*Edmund Hollier*

Windsor Castle Mincemeat 112
*The Court Chef, Alexis Soyer, 1861*

'Winter Sports' 113
*Anon*

The Mummers 116
*From Thomas Hardy's* The Return of the Native

Cornish Cakes and Other Customs 124
*From* Christmas in Cornwall Sixty Years Ago
*Mrs John Bonham*

'The Ballade of Christmas Ghosts' 130
*Andrew Lang*

Reminiscences of Christmas 131
*From* Sketches by 'Boz', *Charles Dickens*

Candied Walnuts, English Caramels and
Preserved Violets 138
*Recipes for sweets from* Home Notes, *1898*

'A Fenland Carol' 140
*Rudyard Kipling*

'Christmas Eve' 141
*Ruth and Celia Duffin*

'The Wondrous Tree of Christmas' 143
*Glyn Griffiths*

Village Christmas 149
*Cyril Palmer*

Nativity Play 154
*Iris Cannon*

All Aboard for Santa's Grotto 158
*Maria Hubert*

A Christmas Epilogue 163
*William Makepeace Thackeray*

*Sources and Bibliography* 166

*Acknowledgements* 168

Catching the stage – going home for Christmas.

# The Great British Christmas –
# An Introduction

## Maria Hubert

*For many, the British Christmas is the epitome of Christmas. Visitors travel from all over the world just to be in Britain and to be able to appreciate the atmosphere of a British Christmas.*

Many of the innovations of Christmas that are enjoyed around the world today originated in Britain. The Christmas card, invented by Henry Cole and his friend the engraver John Horsley in 1843, was to become the means in a great many countries of showing distant friends that they were remembered. The Christmas cracker, a toy created by the confectioner Tom Smith in 1840 and which later received the royal warrant, has become an essential part of Christmas celebrations. The Christmas tree was, of course, a German custom. However, in the 1840s the tree found favour with fashionable society after the *Illustrated London News* published the now famous engraving of Queen Victoria and her consort Prince Albert with their children around the Christmas tree at Windsor.

People in many countries recognise the name Charles Dickens and are familiar with his story *A Christmas*

A steel engraving depicting Christmas being celebrated in a sixteenth-century English baronial hall.

*Carol*. During the war years, the Dickensian Christmas was portrayed as an ideal, creating a nostalgic longing in everyone. Christmas cards showed ladies in crinolines and gentlemen in Dickensian frock-coats shopping at bulls-eye paned shops. The British Christmas is also associated with white Christmas – snow, snowball fights, tobogganing on the new red sledge brought by Father Christmas, skating on icy ponds, carolling. Strangely, although we can all remember a white Christmas, it very rarely snows on Christmas Eve or Day!

From the earliest times, Britain has celebrated Christmas. The early christianised Romans who settled in the Welsh Borders brought with them the custom of Strenia, the giving of gifts from the groves of the Roman goddess, Strenia, which bought good fortune to all who received them. This became the Welsh Calennig, which is still given in small areas along the borderlands today. The Norsemen brought their sun breads and corn meal to Scotland and the north of England. Today, these have become Scottish shortbread, the segments of which represent the traditional image of the sun's rays, and the Yorkshire 'moggy', a wheaten porridge served to break the fast on Christmas Eve and which is still occasionally eaten in isolated areas.

# *Christmas Books*

## William Makepeace Thackeray

*Christmas books were a feature of the nineteenth century. They were small books designed to be given as presents and released by publishers hoping to catch Christmas sales. However, Christmas books rarely contained anything of a seasonal nature, which prompted that observer of social custom William Makepeace Thackeray to write an essay on the subject.*

*Thackeray wrote extensively on the theme of Christmas, among other subjects, and not one part of this festival escaped his wry humour from the expense of children's parties to the frivolity of the pantomime. He himself created a series of Christmas books which he had published during the 1840s and 1850s. It is not surprising perhaps that the following essay was encouraged by the rather scathing press he received for one of his Christmas books.* The Times *no less, which distressed Thackeray so, accused all writers and publishers of Christmas books of being scavengers, no better than the*

*dustman knocking for his Christmas box! It is presented here, in an*
*abridged form, as a tongue-in-cheek amusement by one such*
*scavenger of Christmas boxes!*

## Being an Essay on Thunder and Small Beer

Any reader who may have a fancy to purchase a copy of this present second edition of the *History of the Kickleburys Abroad*, had best be warned in time that *The Times* newspaper does not approve of the work, and has but a bad opinion both of the author and his readers. Nothing can be fairer than this statement: if you happen to take up the poor little volume at a railroad station, and read this sentence, lay the book down, and buy something else. You are warned. What more can the author say? If after this you *will* buy, – amen! Pay your money, take your book, and fall to. Between ourselves, honest reader, it is no very strong potation which the present purveyor offers to you. It will not trouble your head much in the drinking.

It was intended for that sort of negus which is offered at Christmas parties; and of which ladies and children may partake with refreshment and cheerfulness. Last year I tried a brew which was old, bitter, and strong; and scarce any one would drink it. This year we send round milder tap, and it is liked by customers: though the critics (who like strong ale, the rogues!) turn up their noses. Heaven's name, Mr. Smith, serve round the liquor to the gentlefolks. Pray, dear Madam, another glass; it is Christmas time: it will do you no harm. It is not intended to keep, this sort of drink. (Come, froth up, Mr. Publisher, and – quickly round!) And as for the professional gentlemen, we must get a stronger sort for *them* some day.

*The Times* gentleman (a very difficult gent to please) is the loudest and noisiest of all, and has made more hideous over the refreshment offered to him than any other critic. There is no use shirking this statement: when a man has been abused in *The Times*, he can't hide it, any more than he could hide the knowledge of his having been committed to prison by Mr. Henry, or publicly caned in Pall Mall. You see it in your friends' eyes when they meet you. They know it. They have chuckled over it to a man. They whisper about it at the club, and look over the paper at you. My next-door neighbour came to see me this morning, and I saw by his face that he had the whole story pat. 'Hem!' says he, 'well, I *have* heard of it; and the fact is, they were talking about you at dinner last night, and mentioning that *The Times* had – ahem! – "walked into you."'

Here is *The Times* piece:

It has been customary of late years for the purveyors of amusing literature – the popular authors of the day – to put forth certain opuscules denominated 'Christmas Books' with the ostensible intention of swelling the tide of exhilaration, or other expansive emotions, incident upon the exodus of the old and the inauguration of the new year.

We have said that their intention was such because there is another motive for these productions . . . Oh that any muse should be cast upon a high stool to cast up accounts and balance a ledger! Yet it is so. And the popular author finds it convenient to fill up the declared deficit!, and place himself in the position the more effectually to encounter those liabilities which sternly assert themselves contemporaneously and in contrast with the careless and freehanded tendencies of the season by the emission of Christmas books – a kind of literary '*assignats*' representing to the emitter expunged debts, to the receiver an investment of enigmatical value. For the most part wearing the stamp of their origin in the vacuity of the writer's exchequer rather than in the fullness of his genius, they suggest by their feeble flavour the rinsings of a void brain after the more portant concoctions of the expired year. Indeed, we should as little think of taking these compositions as examples of the merits of their authors as we should think of measuring the valuable services of Mr. Walker, the postman, or Mr. Bell, the dust-collector, by the copy of verses they leave at our doors as a provocative of the expected annual gratuity-effusions with which they may fairly be classed for their intrinsic worth no less than their ultimate purport.

. . . I suppose you and I had to announce the important news that some writers published what are called Christmas books; that Christmas books are so called because they are published at Christmas; and that the purpose of the authors is to try and amuse people. Suppose, I say, we had, by the sheer force of intellect, or by other means of observation or information, discovered these great truths, we should have announced them in so many words. And there it is that the difference lies between a great writer and a poor one; and we may see how an inferior man may fling a chance away.

. . . The popular author finds it convenient to fill up the declared deficit by the emission of Christmas books – a kind of *assignats* that bear the stamp of their origin in the *vacuity* of the writer's exchequer. There is a trope for you! You rascal, you wrote because you wanted money! His lordship has found out what you were at, and that there is a deficit in your till. But he goes on to say that we poor devils are to be pitied in our necessity; and that these compositions are no more to be taken as examples of our merits than the verses which the dustman leaves at his lordship's door 'as a provocative of the expected annual gratuity,' are to be considered as measuring his, the scavenger's, valuable services – nevertheless the author's and the scavenger's 'effusions may fairly be classed, for *their* intrinsic worth, no less than their ultimate purport.'

Heaven bless his lordship on the bench – What a gentlemanlike badinage he has, and what a charming and playful wit always at hand! What a sense he has for a simile, O what Mrs. Malaprop calls an odorous comparison, and how gracefully he conducts it to 'its ultimate purport'. Gentleman writing a poor little book is a scavenger asking for a Christmas box!

But when this profound scholar compares me to a scavenger who leaves a copy of verses at his door and begs Christmas-box, I must again cry out, and say, 'My air, it is true your simile is offensive, but can you make it? Are you not hasty in your figures and allusions?'

. . . How can I be like a dustman that rings for a Christmas box at your hall-door? I never was there in my life. I never left at your door a copy of verses provocative of an annual gratuity, as your noble honour styles it. Who are you? If you are the man I take you to be, it must have been you who asked the publisher for my book, and not I who sent it in, and begged a gratuity of your worship. You abused me out of *The Times'* window; but if ever your noble honour sent me a gratuity out of your own door, may I never drive another dust-cart. 'Provocative of a gratuity!' O splendid swell! How much was it your worship sent out to me by the footman? Every farthing you have paid I will restore to your lordship, and I swear I shall not be a halfpenny the poorer.

As before, and on similar seasons and occasions, I have compared myself to a person following a not dissimilar calling, let me suppose now, for a minute, that I am a writer of a Christmas farce, who sits in the pit, and sees the performance of his own piece. There comes applause, hissing, yawning, laughter, as may be; but the loudest critic of all is our friend the cheap buck, who sits yonder and makes his remarks, so that all the audience may hear. '*This* a farce!' says Beau Tibbs; 'demmy! it's the work of a poor devil who writes for money, confound his vulgarity! This a farce! Why isn't it a tragedy, or a comedy, or an epic poem, stap my vitals? This is a farce, indeed! It's a feller as sends round his 'at, and appeals to charity.

Let's 'ave our money back again, I say.' And he swaggers off; – and you find the fellow came with an author's order.

But if, in spite of Tibbs, our 'kynd friends,' &c-&c-&c., – if the little farce, which was meant to amuse

Christmas (or what my classical friend calls Exodus), is asked for, even up to Twelfth Night, – shall the publishers stop because Tibbs is dissatisfied? Whenever that capitalist calls to get his money back, he may see the letter from the respected publisher, informing the author that all the copies are sold, and that there are demands for a new edition. Up with the curtain, then! Vivat Regina! and no money returned except *The Times'* 'gratuity'.

M.A. TITMARSH.
January 5 1851

# *The Calennig*

*During the Roman occupation of Britain many customs from the old Roman Empire were adopted and changed to suit the lifestyles of the early Christians. One such custom evolved from the giving of Branches of Peace and Good Fortune in honour of the Roman deity, Strenia. The Calennig, which is a New Year gift, is an apple with nuts and raisins pressed into it, a sprig of greenery placed in the top and three twig legs which form a*

Traditional Welsh Borders' Calennig.

*stand. The children would go around the houses giving these gifts to their family and friends and neigbours. The apples were usually kept on the windowsill for good luck throughout the year. The custom more or less died out in the 1950s and 1960s. A translation of a Welsh carol sung by the children who delivered this gift is reproduced here.*

Calennig for me, Calennig for the stick
Calennig to eat this evening
Calennig for my dad for mending my shoe
Calennig for my mam for sewing my sock.

Well, this is the Calend, remember the day
And give free a Calennig from your heart,
If you give free on the first day of the year
Without fail every day will be blessed.

Calennig for the Master, Calennig for the boy
Calennig for the girl who lives in the big house
Calennig for the man and Calennig for his wife
Calennig of money to all scholars!

# *King Arthur's Christmas*

## Sir Thomas Malory

*There is a legend, preserved in Sir Thomas Malory's* Morte d'Arthur, *published by Caxton in 1485, that Arthur pulled the sword from the stone on Christmas Day. The date is dubious, but it was during the sixth century. Below is an extract from Malory, which has been anglicised to make it more accessible to the modern reader.*

'The fair sword in the stone' by Jung Sook Nam.

. . . Then Merlin went to the Archbishop of Canterbury, and counselled him for to send for all the lords of the Realm, and all the gentlemen of arms, that they should come to London by Christmas, upon pain of cursing and for this cause, that Jesus that was born on that night, would of his great mercy shew some miracle, as he was come to be king of mankind, to shew who would be rightful king of this realm. So the Archbishop, by the advice of Merlin, sent for all the Lords that they should come by Christmas unto London. And make of them clean of their life [shriven by a priest in the sacrament of Confession], that their prayer might be more acceptable to God . . . And when matins and the First Mass [of Christmas] was done, there was seen in the churchyard, against the High Altar, a great stone four square . . . and therein stuck a fair sword . . . and letters there were written in gold about the stone that said thus:

Whoso pulleth out this sword of this stone and anvil, is rightwise king born of all England . . . But none might stir the sword nor use it . . .

So upon New Year's Day, when the service was done, the barons rode unto the field, some to joust, some to tourney, and so it happened that Sir Ector . . . rode unto the joust, and with him rode Sir Kay his son, and young Arthur that was his nourished brother. . . . Sir Kay lost his sword for he had left it at his father's lodging, and so he prayed young Arthur to ride for his sword. . . . Then Arthur said to himself, I will take the sword that sticketh in the stone . . . so he handled the sword by the handles, and lightly and fiercely pulled it out from the stone . . . and rode his way until he came to Sir Kay and delivered him the sword. Sir Kay saw the sword and knew it well as the sword in the stone . . . therewithal they went unto the archbishop, and told him how the sword was achieved, and by whom; and on Twelfth-Day all the barons came thither, and to try to take the sword, who that would try. But there afore them all there might none take it out but Arthur.

# 'Eddi's Service'

## Rudyard Kipling

*Based on an old Sussex legend, Kipling's poem 'Eddi's Service' retells this story of the Spirit of Christmas. It was originally written as 'The Conversion of St Wilfred' from Rewards and Fairies in 1910.*

Eddi, priest of St Wilfred,
In his chapel at Manhood End,
Ordered a midnight service
For such as cared to attend.

But the Saxons were keeping Christmas,
And the night was stormy as well,
Nobody came to service,
Though Eddi rang the bell.

'Wicked weather for walking'
Said Eddi of Manhood End,
'But I must go on with the service
For such as care to attend.'

The altar lamps were lighted –
An old marsh donkey came,
Bold as a guest invited,
And stared at the guttering flame.

'Three are gathered together'
by Jung Sook Nam.

The storm beat on at the windows,
The water splashed on the floor,
And a wet, yoke-weary Bullock
Pushed in through the open door.

'How do I know what is greatest,
How do I know what is least?
That is my Father's business,'
Said Eddi, Wilfred's priest.

'But – three are gathered together –
Listen to me and attend.
I bring good news, my brethren!'
Said Eddi, of Manhood End.

And he told the Ox of a Manger
And a stall in Bethlehem.
And he spoke to the Ass of a Rider
That rode to Jerusalem.

They steamed and dripped in the chancel,
They listened and never stirred,
While, just as though they were Bishops,
Eddi preached them the Word.

Till the gale blew off on the marshes,
And the windows showed the day,
And the Ox and the Ass together
Wheeled and clattered away.

And when the Saxons mocked him,
Said Eddi of Manhood End
'I dare not shut His chapel
For such as care to attend.'

# 'The First Wassail'

## R. Acton

*The legend that the tradition of the wassail came from a peacemaking
feast between the British chieftain Vortigern and the invading Saxon
Hengist is told in the epic poem 'The First Wassail', by R. Acton. The
toast at the celebration was 'Wachts heil!' meaning 'grow healthy',
and from this we get the word 'Wassail'. The story of Vortigern and
Hengist and Horsa is true and dates from the fifth century.*

## Part One

'Twas fourteen hundred years ago, and twenty years
  beside,
The thing of which fly verse shall tell in Britain did
  betide,
When Vortigern, the British chief, had got the full
  command,
The sons of Roman Constantine had driven from the
  land.

The bitter North sent forth its swarms, across the Roman
  wall
For plunder leagued, the Scots and Picts, on this good
  land to fall,
While from beyond the southern sea, on Brittany's far
  shore,
Ambrose and Uther, princes wronged, a vengeful purpose
  bore.

So Vortigern was sore perplexed, till as he paced one day
The eastward cliff where Ramsgate is, he looked o'er
  Pegwell Bay,
And saw three ships of foreign shape the narrow channel
  gain
Between the Isle of Thanet there, and Kentish land the
  main.

The herald of King Vortigern was sent in haste to know
What strangers made so bold to come, and if as friend or
  foe;

And soon he brought their answer back, 'We're Saxons
    wild and free,
We seek a richer home than ours – we mean to dwell
    with thee.'

Beyond the Weser and the Elbe, towards the Baltic coast,
In Holstein, Schleswig, Jutland too, were reared the
    sturdy host
Of Saxons, Jutes, and Angles all, who long through
    Britain ranged,
Until its native Celtic race, for English folk was changed.

But Vortigern was ignorant, as man will ever be,
Of changes near and distant hid in dark futurity,
With Hengist and with Horsa then, twin captains of the
    crew
He met in talk and questioned them of ways and manners
    new.
These heathens, who the Church and faith of Christendom
    ignored,
Their Woden, Freya, Saturn, Thor on weekly days
    adored.

They sought to win a wealthy land by work of sword
    and spear;
For this their nation sent a fleet in every seventh year.
'Now welcome, valiant Saxons' did the King of Britain say;
'I bid you fight to save my realm, and well I will you pay,
For service of your sword and spear in land of soil the
    best,

My foes shall be defeated then, my kingdom be at rest.'
They struck the bargain there, and soon they marched
   into the North;
The Saxons beat the Picts and Scots from Humber,
   Tweed and Forth;
To Hengist, son of Woden, did King Vortigern allow
Near half the shire of Lincoln, as we call the county now.

The Lindsey Portion was the land he held by such a
   claim;
The Lindis River – Witham now – gave Lindis-Ey its
   name,
Whence northward to the Humber tide, and westward to
   the Trent;
And eastward to the open sea, the Saxons province went.

Too large and wide a land, I ween, was this for men so few;
But Hengist nigh to Vortigern with crafty counsel drew,
And said, 'Thy foes in Brittany I bid thee to beware,
Or let me send for Saxons more, and thy defence prepare.'
Now Vortigern, an idle King, who reigned the State to mar,
Was heedless of his business, of policy and war,
Of hunting and of hawking, of feasting and of drinking,
Of gallantry and ladies gay he rather would be thinking.

This foolish monarch gave constant Hengist did him say,
So eighteen ships to Botolph's town, did presently convey
A chosen troop of Saxon men all clad in coats of mail,
With iron helms and shields and spears and swords that
   would not fail.

On Lindis bank they leap to land; 'proud Hengist waits
  his own';
They shout for joy, now close. Their ranks the brazen
  trumpet blown;
The White Horse banner, waving high, delights their
  eager eyes;
A clang of arms begins their march; the road far inland lies.

### Part Two

Some twenty miles from Lincoln, high, upon the middle
  hill
Is Caistor, now a market town; you go there if you will.
There Hengist, Karl of Saxons, built his castle big and
  strong
Measured its site with hide of ox he cut to strips of
  thong.

(No that's the tale of Carthage) so we scout the stale old
  fable
Where Hengist, lord of Lindsey, chose to build, he sure
  was able.
I doubt not that his 'Thongcastle' had room enough to
  hold
Five hundred of the Saxon chiefs, his fellows stout and
  bold.

Earl Hengist, when his mansion new was ready for good
  living,
Bethought him of a housewarming and dinner-party
  giving;

The wassail feast, a pen and ink drawing by W.F. Dawson, 1902.

King Vortigern, then hunting near, his frequent recreation,
To come and dine and take a bed received an invitation.

The spacious hall of Hengist's home was full of pomp
  and glee,
Where burly Saxons, lively Celts, were met for revelry.
Hung on the wall their weapons sharp of battle and of
  chase,
While all the guests on benches sat, in order due of place.

No Christian priest or chaplain said a grace at Hengist's
  board,
To Woden and to Freya he profane libation poured;
In trenchers vast uncovered lay the sides of roasted swine,
Roast oxen cut in quarters, meat for giants set to dine.

Huge piles of bread the master sent to all his guests
  aright,
Their platters heaped, they drew their knives, they ate
  with stern delight,

They drank with joy, in crystal cups, the wine of finest
  cheer,
In mugs and horns the honey-mead, in wooden tubs the
  beer.

But when the fatness of the feast, and drink that heats
  the blood,
Made all their hearts beat strong and fast, Lord Hengist
  rose and stood:
'My Harper! Strike thy tuneful strings! Let music rouse
  the soul!
My Daughter comes! ROWENA brings our Royal Guest
  the Bowl!'

The first wassail cup, a steel engraving by Hennessy, 1871.

Loud through the house of Hengist rang the harp and trump and song;

In at the open door She came, the mailed knights among;

Down on the rushy floor She knelt before the Briton's chair,

In robe of purple velvet clad; a lady free and fair.

Her lip was like the cherry red, her face was rosy bright,

Like summer sky her eye was blue, her hair was sunny light,

As princess or as queen She wore a golden diadem,

She bore a golden goblet set with many a precious gem.

'LIEF KING WACHS HEIL!' the Maiden cried; the ruddy wine She quaffed.

'WACHS HEIL!' each Saxon throat exclaimed, and took its jolly draught.

'WACHS HEIL!' the puzzled Britons asked, 'What means this Saxon word?'

Then Hengist rising, cup in hand, to tell its use was heard.

'King of Great Britain, Vortigern and worthy Britons all!

The speech of my Rowena here on friendly ears should fall,

Though uttered with a foreign tongue, in syllables uncouth,

I shall interpret what she says, with voice and heart of truth.

"Dear King, thy health!" or "Grow in health!" for that's
  about the sense,
The very phrase is just WAX HALE! I hope there's no
  offence?
Do thou in courtesy reply, DRINK, HEIL! and drink it up,
This custom of our Saxon race attends the social cup.'

'I like your jovial custom well,' King Vortigern replied;
'Hengist, I love this princely maid; I ask her for my
  bride.'
'Done!' said her father instantly. The question put and
  carried,
Rowena to King Vortigern that very night was married.

### Part Three

The longest and the sweetest night will have a morn of
  waking,
And Vortigern was roused from sleep when early day
  was breaking;
His father-in-law Hengist came, and stood beside his
  bed,
'Good-morrow, Royal Son! I crave the "MORNING
  GIFT"' he said.

'The custom of our Saxon folk allows my certain right
To ask what boon I will of you, when passed your
  wedding night;
I ask the Isle of Thanet now, and all the Kentish land,
From Medway's marsh to Dover fort, to have in my
  command.'

'Nay, by Saint Alban!' said the King, 'Too large a gift to
  choose!'
Queen Rowena looked at him; the fool could not refuse.
That day to Thanet Horsa rode, with men of Hengist's
  train,
And letters from King Vortigern, a province new to gain.

I'm sorry for King Vortigern; I pity him the more
For just a little circumstance he'd quite forgot before,
In haste to wed the Pagan maid – forgot his tie for life,
Forgot his three tall manly sons, his living Christian wife.

Of her, this lawful wife and Queen, I've nothing more to
  say;
She went into a nunnery, to weep if not to pray;
Of Vortimer, of Catigern, of Pasigen, we are told
Brave deeds of war recorded in the chronicles of old.

The brothers three in British hearts a purpose cherished
  long,
They would amend their father's shame, and right their
  nation's wrong;
In Troynovant Prince Vortimer was held the best of names,
And where the Exe and Severn flow, as on the banks of
  Thames.

Hengist persuaded Vortigern, by flattery and guile,
To undertake another war, and conquer all the isle;
For which a larger Saxon host of bandits well assorted,
By Hengist's son and brother led, was presently imported.

The Britons wouldn't stand it now; they made a revolution,
Deposed unworthy Vortigern, reformed the Constitution; –
Chose Vortimer to be their King, took weapons in their hands,
And drove the Saxons out of Kent to lie on Goodwin Sands.

The victories of Vortimer are famous yet in story,
At Crayford and at Aylsford he revived the British glory,
Smote off the head of Horsa, sank a fleet beneath the wave;
But malice of a woman brought this hero to the grave.

The poison that Rowena mixed was seething in his blood;
Spoke Vortimer to all the chiefs who weeping round him stood:
'I bid you burn my body soon, and then my ashes take,
A hollow statue like to me of bronze I bid you make;

'I bid you raise it on the cliff above our eastern shore,
'Twill fright the Saxons from this isle, their ships may come no more.'
The hero died. His spirit fled. The fickle Britons' whim
Let Vortigern return to reign, with Hengist ruling him.

*Part Four*

To the beginning of the end I bring my story now;
A little longer patience have, that I may tell you how
On treacherous Rowena Queen, and Vortigern the weak,
Deservedly their fate at last did retribution wreak.

The Saxons still arriving in their thousands year by year,
The British chiefs and Vortigern began to have a fear,
They said to Hengist, 'Send back half!' 'Which half?' did
  Hengist say,
'I know not whom you wish to keep and whom to send
  away'
'I'll tell you what,' said Hengist then, 'when May brings
  summer weather,
At Amesbury, on Sarum Plain, I'll place my men together,
Where you, my British friends, shall see my harmless
  Saxons stand,
And choose ye some to serve your King – some to quit
  your land.'

The silly Britons and their King into his trap did fall;
On May Day next, at Amesbury, they met the Saxons all;
Nor spear nor sword the Saxon had, but hidden in their
  hose
The horrid knives they seaxen called, in use to stab their
  foes.
Seeming unarmed, the Saxon host was orderly reviewed;
His peaceful promise with oaths Earl Hengist there
  renewed;
Then bade the Britons sit and dine, but to his Saxons spoke
'Nehmt eure Seaxen' said the Earl, and out the Murder
  broke!

The Saxons with their seaxen sharp, their daggers dealing
  death,
Four hundred British noblemen soon laid upon the heath,

Yet Eidiol, Lord of Gloucester, with no weapon but a
   pole,
Killing seventy of the Saxons, saved his life and body
   whole.

This slaughter spared King Vortigern, for wily Hengist
   meant
Rowena still should sway his mind to ev'ry bad intent,
And Vortigern dissembled first, but afterwards he fled,
And in a castle on the Wye got cover for his head.

The Saxons harried all the land, the people's goods
   distrained
The churches burnt, the clergy killed, the tombs of saints
   profaned;
Till from the shore of Brittany Ambrose and Uther
   sailing
To set this isle of Britain free, came with a force
   prevailing.

Hard Hengist they defeated soon, and slew beyond the
   Trent,
To the castle on the Wye for Vortigern they went;
They girt the house with brands of flame and wrought
   their fierce desire:
Rowena died with Vortigern in that avenging fire!

# A Horn of Mead

## Anon

Here is my recipe for mead, that ancient beverage which it is said the Vikings drank from cattle horns. Homemade mead is not necessarily a strong drink, though it is alcoholic.

In my opinion mead is better drunk fairly fresh while it still has the delicate honey flavour. The recipe is very simple. It can, if liked, be used immediately, but it takes a few days for the sparkle to develop.

A Christmas toast in seventeenth-century England, Vizelly Brothers, 1840.

8 quarts water; 2 pounds honey; 1 lemon; 1 pint pale ale; ¼ teaspoon bread yeast; a few raisins; a little sugar.

Bring water to boil in large preserving pan. Dissolve honey in it. Peel lemon thinly, remove pith, slice fruit, take away pips, put slices and rind into pan. Turn off heat, leave till almost cold. Add ale and yeast dissolved in a little tepid water. Leave to stand overnight. Strain mead into bottles adding two washed raisins or sultanas to each bottle with a teaspoon of sugar. It is easiest to use bottles with screw tops, but if you use corks tie them down securely or they will eventually pop out after half a day in warm room; store in cool dark place for a week.

There is usually a little sediment at the bottom of the bottles, so they should be handled carefully when you pour out the mead.

# An Anglo-Norman Carol

*According to* Christmas with the Poets, *a volume of seasonal verse and its history published in 1840, one of the earliest sung carols is that known as 'The Anglo-Norman Carol'. It is said to have been found on a manuscript dating from the thirteenth century, and was thought to have belonged to a group of travelling troubadours. The publisher's modern English transcription is reproduced here.*

Lordlings, listen to our lay –
We have come from far away
To seek Christmas;
In this mansion we are told

Minstrels in the twelfth century, Vizelly Brothers, 1840.

He his yearly feast doth hold:
'Tis to day!
May joy come from God above
To all those who Christmas love!

Lordlings, I now tell you true,
Christmas bringeth unto you
Only mirth;
His house he fills with many a dish
Of bread and meat and also fish,
To grace the day.
May joy come from God above,
To all these who Christmas love.

Lordlings through our army's band
They say – who spends with open hand
Free and fast,
And oft regales his many friends –
God gives him double what he spends,
To grace the day,
May joy come from God above,
To all those who Christmas love.

Lordlings, wicked men eschew,
In them never shall you view
Aught thats good;
Cowards are the rabble rout,
Kick and beat the grumblers out,
To grace the day.
May joys come from God above,
To all them who Christmas love.

To English ale, and Gascon wine,
And French, doth Christmas much incline –
And Anjou's, too;
He makes his neighbour freely drink,

So that in sleep his head doth sink
Often by day.
May joys flow from God above,
To all those who Christmas love.

Lords, by Christmas and the host
Of this mansion hear my toast –
Drink it well –
Each must drain his cup of wine,
And I the first will toss off mine;
Thus I advise,
Here then, I bid you all Wassail,
Cursed be who will not say 'Drinkhail'.

# The Second Shepherd's Play

*In the Middle Ages religious dramas were acted out, usually by the guildsmen and more honoured townsfolk, and related stories from the Bible. These plays were originally part of the Church liturgy but eventually became secularised. The extract reproduced here is from the 'Second Shepherd's Play', which originated in Wakefield, Yorkshire, during the fourteenth century. It tells of the Angel bringing the Glad Tidings to three very rough and ignorant shepherds. The shepherds have just arrived at the Stable in Bethlehem.*

**1st Shepherd**
Hail, comely and clean; hail young child!
Hail! Maker, as I mean, of a maiden so mild!

Thou hast warned off I ween, of the warlock so wild,
The false guiler of men, now goes he beguiled.
Lo, He laughs, my sweeting,
A welcome meeting!
I have given my greeting
Have a bob of cherries?

**2nd Shepherd**

Hail, sovereign Saviour, for thou hast us sought!
Hail, freely, leaf and flower,
That all things hath wrought.
Hail, full of favour, that made all of nought!
Hail! I kneel and I cower. A bird have I brought
To my bairn!
Hail, little tiny mop,
Of our creed thou art crop!
I would drink in thy cup
Little day-starn.

**3rd Shepherd**

Hail! darling dear. Full of Godhead!
I pray thee be near, when I have need.
Hail! Sweet is thy cheer; my heart would bleed
To see thee sit here in so poor weed.
With no pennies.
Hail! Put forth thy paw! –
I bring thee but a ball
Have and play thee with all
And go to the tennis.

# A Hue and Cry After Christmas

## Simon Minc'd Pye

Seventeenth-century broadsheet by Simon Minc'd Pye.

*In 1645 Christmas was banned by Parliament! What a dreadful day that must have been for the people. Records reveal that there were riots in Canterbury, soldiers were employed to sniff out the baking of spicy Christmas pies, printers secretly published works which decried the Acts of Parliament and Christmas went underground. One famous broadsheet was published and distributed by a man who called himself, seasonally, Simon Minc'd Pye, and his address included all the banned foods and games of Christmas! It reads as follows:*

The Arraignment, conviction and imprisonment of CHRISTMAS on St Thomas' Day last. AND
How he broke out of prison in the Holidayes and got away, onely left his hoary hair, and grey beard, sticking between two Iron bars of a window. WITH

A Hue and Cry after Christmas, and a letter from Mr Wood-cock, an fellow in Oxford, to a Malignant Lady in London. And divers passages between the Lady and the Cryer, about Old Christmas: And what Shift he was fain to make to save his life, and great stir to fetch him back again. With divers other Witty Passages

Printed by Simon Minc'd Pye for Cissily Plum-Porridge; and are to be sold by Ralph Fidler, Chandler, at the signe of the Pack of Cards, Mustard Alley, in Brawn Street. 1645.

*This tract was supposedly a reaction to 'a letter from Mr Woodcock, a fellow in Oxford, to a Malignant Lady in London':*

Lady,

I beseech you, for the love of Oxford, hire a Cryer (I will see him paid for his paines) to cry Old Father Christmas, and keep him with you (if you can meet with him, and stay him) till we come to London, for we expect to be there shortly, and then we will have all things are they were wont, I warrant you; hold up your spirits, and let not your old friend be lost out of your favour, for his sake who is

your ever servant, Jo Woodcock

# 'Old Christmas Still Comes!'

*Following the 'Hue and Cry After Christmas' during the seventeenth century, it seemed that Britain would never again wish to lose sight of his hoary old head. However, the latter years of the twentieth century*

*have proved otherwise, and Christmas is once more under attack as*
*religious extremists try to discredit the celebration of Christmas. The*
*following anonymous poem tells the whole history of Christmas in*
*the traditional sense. Christmas' customary challenge, when he*
*appeared in the seventeenth century, was a taunt to the soldiers:*
*'In comes I Old Father Christmas! Be I welcome or be I not, I hopes*
*that Old Christmas will ne'er be forgot!'*

'Where is that hoary headed gent' the Hue and Cry for
    Christmas went
When soldiers were chose for the skill of their nose
To sniff out Christmas pies and report.
For when Christmas was banned, men were spying on spies,
And Young lads hid their footballs inside.

'Old Christmas comes to the home', an artist's impression of a medieval Father
Christmas, Warne, 1870.

Christmas Day was for working – and shops raised their
  blinds, and all praise and playing despised.

Yet Sir Christmas did come, welcome or not, to villages,
  houses and hall,
He was sure of his case, and all danger did face –
  and his challenge he loudly did call!

In times long ago as a god he did ride on a white horse of
  singular speed
O'er the great northern skies, and the people would cry
'There he goes on his eight-legged steed!'
Then to earth he would fall, don a cloak with a cowl,
And around all his lands did he go
For to sit by the fires and listen awhile, to hear all the
  tales of men's woe.

For Christe-mas comes, welcome or not, to villages,
  fireside and hall,
He was sure of his case, and all danger did face –
  and his challenge he loudly did call!

As a Saint he was hailed from the East to the West, friend
  of children and sailors, and all
Who, in eye of the storm, or of poverty born, cried
'St Nicholas please hear our call!'
Then his prayer quelled the seas, or a coin left to please,
His fame rode on their stories worldwide.
And as saint of the seas, a ship's figurehead he, to the
New World set sail on the tide.

Old Christmas and his family,
R. Seymour, 1836.

For Christe-mas comes,
welcome or not, to the
children, the sailor, the poor,
He was sure of his case, every
danger he faced –
and his challenge he loudly
did roar!

In the modern day world he
still comes on his round – but
his memory is fading away,
Fewer children watch out for
his sleigh, fewer shout
'Father Christmas is coming this way'
He who changed from a god to a saint and survived all
of Cromwell's infernal decrees
Is reduced to a fat ineffectual old man, who tries, oh so
hard, still to please.

For Old Christe-mas still comes, welcome or not, to the
village, the town and the hall,
Now not sure of his case, but his challenge still makes
But his voice is incredibly small.

Revive him we must! For in him is the trust
Of all our belief in mankind.
His world it grows larger, encompasses farther –
To children of various kind.
Brings the world close together, regardless of whether
They are people of different mind.

For Old Christmas still comes for whatever it's worth,
To the children all over the earth
And regardless of pedigree, 'Tis certain he'll always be
The symbol of 'Goodwill on Earth'.

# *Christmas with the Diarists*

## Samuel Pepys, John Evelyn and Others

*Many Christmas traditions are remembered today because prominent
citizens, authors and clergymen recorded them in their diaries and
other written sources. These texts allow us to build up pictures of the
food, pastimes and revels that formed Christmas celebrations in
previous centuries. There follow several short written extracts from
the seventeenth through to the nineteenth century.*

*John Evelyn, Christmas 1644*

On Christmas-Eve at night I went not to bed, my reason
that I was desirous to see the many extraordinary
Ceremonyes perform'd then in Their Churches, as midnight *Masses, &* Sermons; so as I did nothing all this
night but go from Church to Church in admiration at
The multitude of sceanes, and pageantry which The
Friars had with all industry & craft set out to catch the
devout women and superstitious sort of people with,
who never part from them without dropping some mony
in a vessell set on purpose: But especially observable was

The pupetry in the Church of the Minerva, representing the nativity &c: thence I went and heard a Sermon at the Appollinare by which time it was morning.

On Christmas day his holynesse sa[y]ing Masse, the Artillery at St Angelo went off: and all this day was exposed the Cradle of our Lord.

27 A great Supper is given the poore at The Hosp: of S: Jo: Laterno

29 We were invited by the English Jesuites to dinner being their greate feast of Tho: of Canterbury: We din'd in their common Refectory, and afterward saw an Italian Comedy Acted by their Alumni before The Cardinals.

*John Evelyn, Christmas 1657*

25 I went with my Wife &c: to Lond: to celebrate Christmas day Mr Gunning preaching in Excester Chapell on 7:Micha 2. Sermon ended, as he was giving us the holy Sacrament, The Chapell was surrounded with Souldiers: All the Communicants and Assembly surpriz'd & kept Prisoners by them, some in the house, others carried away: It fell to my share to be confined to a roome in the house, where yet were permitted to Dine with the master of it, the Countess of Dorset, Lady Hatton & some others of quality who invited me: In the afternoone came Collonel Whaly, Foffe & others from Whitehall to examine us one by one, & some they committed to the Marial, some to Prison, some Committed: When I came before them they tooke my name and aboad, examind me, why contrarie to

an Ordinance made that none should any longer observe the superstitious time of the Nativity (*so* esteem'd by them) I durst offend, & particularly be at Common prayers, which they told me was but the Masse in English, & particularly pray for Charles Stuard, for which we had no scriptures: I told them we did not pray for Cha: Steward but for all Christian Kings, Princes & Govenors; They replied, in so doing we praied for the K. of Spaine too, who was their Enemie, & a Papist, with other frivolous & insnaring questions, with much threatening, & finding no colour to detaine me longer, with much pitty of my Ignorance, they dismiss'd me: These were men of high flight, and above Ordinances: & spake spitefull things of our B: Lords nativity: so I got home late the next day blessed by God: These wretched miscreants, held their muskets against us as we came up to receive the Sacred Elements, as if they would have shot us at the Altar, but yet suffering us to finish the Office of Communion, as perhaps not in their Instructions what they should do in case they found us in that Action:

*Despite the ragings of the Plague, most people continued to lead normal lives, as is revealed in this extract from Samuel Pepys:*

1666, 24th December . . . Lay pretty long in bed then rose leaving my wife desirous to sleep, having sat up till four this morning seeing her mayds make mince-pies. I to church, where our Parson made a good sermon. Then home, and dined well on some good ribbs of Beef roasted and mince pies; only my wife, brother and Barker; and plenty of good wine of my owne, and my heart full of

Calling for a Christmas box, R. Seymour, 1836.

true joy and thanks to Almighty God for the goodness of my condition at this day . . .

*The Christmas box custom whereby tradespeople could call at houses and ask for their Christmas 'tip' to be placed in a clay box modelled from river clay lasted for centuries. Even today, we still tend to give a gift to the postman, refuse collector and various loyal deliverymen. In 1668, Pepys records in slightly exasperated tones,*

Up, called up by drums and trumpets; these things and boxes having cost me much money this Christmas already, and will do more . . .

*In the seventeenth century Christmas ended on the feast of the Purification, 2 February. In the following extract Evelyn tells of a gown worn by the King's mistress Lady Castlemaine, which would compete with the best of today's designer gowns in terms of its value!*

February 2 (candlemas) 1668: I received the Blessed Sacrament; 4 To Lond: This evening I saw the Trajedie of Horace (written by the virtuous Mrs Phillips) acted before their majesties: 'twixt each act a Masque & Antique: daunced. The excessive gallantry of the Ladies was infinite. Those especialy on that . . . Castlemaine esteemed at 40000 pounds and more: and far outshining the Queen.

*The papers of the Duchess of Hamilton during the same period describe the toys available for children in Scotland at Christmas.*

Whenever the Duke visited Edinburgh or London, he would bring back 'bonny things for the bairns', such as toy drums, swords and trumpets, while he had the tailor John Muirhead make gowns for 'the Lady Katherine's doll'. The Scottish merchants were importing large quantities of children's toys into Scotland and one merchant's list reads: 'item: wand rattler [a windmill], item: supple Andrew [possibly what we now call a jumping Jack], item: Leaping Least [possibly a jumping toy], item: Hobby Horse, item: Wagon, item: Timber Crane for a child.'

*Extracts from John Evelyn's diary for December 1683 and January 1684 detail the extremely cold weather conditions and the ice fair that took place on the River Thames.*

It [the Small-pox] was exceedingly mortal at this time; & the season was unsufferably cold. The Thames frozen &c.

25. Christmas day I received the Bl: Sacrament at St James's chapel.

1683/4 January 1 . . . Daughter Susan had some few small pox come forth on her, so as I sent her out of the Family; The Weather continuing intollerably severe, so as streets of Boothes were set upon the Thames &c: and the aire so very cold & thick, as of many yeares there had not been the like:

6. I went home to Says-Court to see my Grandson, it being extreame hard weather, and return'd the next day by Coach the river being quite frozen up:

9. I went crosse the Thames upon the Ice (which was now become so incredibly thick, as to beare not onely whole streets of boothes in which the roasted meate & had divers shops of wares, quite crosse as in a Towne, but Coaches & carts & horses passed over) So I went from Westminster stayers to Lambeth and dined with my L. Archbishop . . . and I returnd, walking over the Ice from Lambeth stayers to the Horse Ferry, and thence walked on foote to our Lodgings:

24. The frost still continuing more & more severe, the Thames before London was planted with bothes in formal streetes, as in a Citty, or Continual faire, all sorts of Trades & shops furnished, & full of Commodities, even to a Printing presse, where People & Ladys tooke a fancy to have their names Printed & the day and yeare set downe, when printed on the Thames:

This humour tooke so universaly, that 'twas estimated the Printer gained five pound a day, for printing a line onely, at six-pence a Name, besides what he got by Ballads &c: Coaches now plied from Westminster to the Temple, & from severall other staires too & froo, as in the streetes; also on sleds, sliding with skeetes; There was likewise Bull-baiting, Horse & Coach races, Pupet-plays & interludes, Cookes & Tipling, & lewder places; so as it seem'd to be a bacchanalia, Triumph or Carnoval on the Water, whilst it was a severe Judgement upon the Land: the Trees not onely splitting as if lightning-strock, but Men & Cattell perishing in divers places, and the very seas so locked up with yce, that no vessells could stirr out, or come in: The fowle (Fish) & birds, & all our exotique Plants & Greens universaly perishing; many Parks of deere destroied, & all sorts of fuell so deare that there were greate Contributions to preserve the poore alive; nor was this severe weather much lesse intense in most parts or Europe even as far as Spaine, & the most southern tracts: London by reason of the excessive coldnesse of the aire, hindring the ascent of the smoke, was so filld with the fuliginous steame of the Sea-Coale, that hardly could one see across the streete. & this filling the lungs with its grosse particles exceedingly obstructed the breast, so as one could scarce breathe: There was no water to be had from the Pipes & Engines, nor could the Brewers, and divers other Tradesmen work, & every moment was full of disasterous accidents &c . . . The frost still raging as fircely as ever, the River of Thames was become a Camp, ten thousands of people, Coaches, Carts, & all manner of sports continuing & increasing: miserable were the wants of poore people.

*By the mid-eighteenth century it had become the custom of many*
*country parsons to invite several poor of the parish to dine with them*
*on Christmas Day. In his diaries, the reverend Mr Woodford describes*
*one such event and also refers to the tradition of having a mince pie*
*for every day of Christmas, Christmas Day being the first day.*

1782. December 25 . . . The following old men dined at my house this day . . . to each besides gave a 1/- [five new pence] in all seven shillings. I gave them for dinner a Surloin of Beef rosted and plenty of plumb-Pudding. We had mince Pies for the first time today.

*Writing his memoirs in 1828, the artist and writer Thomas Bewick*
*records a lively Christmas in Northumberland in his youth.*

1774–76 About Christmas, as I had done before when a boy, I went with my father to a distance to collect the money due to him for his coals. In these rounds I had the opportunity of witnessing the kindness and hospitality of the people. The countenances of all, both high and low, beamed with cheerfulness, and this was heightened everywhere by the music of the old tunes, from the well-known, exhilarating, wild notes of the Northumberland pipes, amidst the buzz occasioned by 'foulpleughs' (morrice or sword dancers) from various parts of the country. This altogether left an impression on my mind which the cares of the world have never effaced from it. The gentry, the farmers, and even the working people had their Christmas home brewed ale, made only from hops and malt.

A Victorian engraving depicting Christmas dinner.

*These seasonal events are best summed up by Charles Dickens in* Sketches by 'Boz', *1832.*

Who can be insensible to the outpourings of good feeling, and the honest interchange of affectionate attachment, which abound at this season of the year? A Christmas family-party! We know nothing more delightful! There seems a magic in the very name of Christmas.

# Deck the Church with Evergreens

## From the *Spectator*

A floral Christmas decoration from *Church Decking*, 1860.

*For many years it was the custom to deck out churches with garlands of evergreens, totally unlike the delicate floral tributes placed on the altar steps today. Parish worthies felt it their bounden duty to plait and weave garlands to trail from pew to pew, to create mottoes and plaques for the walls and great bunches of holly and bay for the tops of pillars. All this was just too much for one young lady who felt obliged to write to the* Spectator *in 1712 on the matter. However, the* Spectator *was renowned for its 'view' on society and inclined to invent its characters for effect – so make of this what you will!*

January 14th 1712

Mr Spectator,

I am a young woman and have my fortune to make, for which reason I am constantly come to church to hear divine service, and make conquests; but one great hindrance in this my design, is that our clerk, who was once a gardener, has this Christmas so over-deckt the church with greens, that he has quite spoilt my prospect, insomuch I have scarce seen the young Baronet I dress at these three weeks, though we

Christmas morning at a country church, R. Seymour, 1836.

have both been very constant at our devotions, and do not sit above three pews off. The church as it is now equipt, looks more like a greenhouse than a place of worship; the middle aisle is a very pretty shady walk, and the pews like so many arbours of each side of it. The pulpit itself has such clusters of ivy, holly, and rosemary about it, that a light fellow in our pews took occasion to say, that the congregation heard the word out of a bush, like Moses. Sir Anthony Love's pew in particular is so well hedged, that all my batteries have no effect. I am obliged to shoot at random among the boughs, without taking any manner of aim. Mr Spectator, unless you will give orders for removing of these greens, I shall grow a very awkward creature at church, and soon have little else to do there but say my prayers.

I am in haste, dear Sir,

Your obedient servant,

Jenny Simper.

# Love and Hot Cockles!

## From the *Spectator*

*Hot cockles was an old parlour game particularly enjoyed by eighteenth-century gentry during the Christmas festivities. One player was required to kneel down with his eyes covered and lay his head in another player's lap. The first player was then struck and had to guess who had dealt the blow. The following letter, which was published in the* Spectator *in 1711, tells us little about the game but perhaps a good deal about the feelings of the housemaid!*

Friday 28 December 1711. Mr Spectator, I am a footman in a great family, and am in love with the housemaid. We were all at Hot Cockles last night, in the hall these holidays; when I lay down and was blinded, she pulled off my shoe, and hit me with the heel with such a rap as almost broke my head to pieces. Pray, Sir, Was this love or spite?

# 'Hallo Hogmanay!'

## D.B. Wyndham Lewis

*'Hallo Hogmanay!' is a short story from a Welsh writer about a Scottish New Year extracted from the quintessentially English* Tatler *magazine in 1952. How British can you get!*

*'Te mann wauk an' Ca' me airly,*
*Ca' me airly, mither, dear,*
*To-morrow'll be the blithest time*
*o' a' the braw New Year,*
*O' a' the braw New Year, mither,*
*the blithest, bonniest show,*
*An' blessin', on your frosty pow,*
*Messrs. John Haig & Co.'*

The girl's clear voice rang out gaily as she unsnid her snood, unbauchled her shoon, lowped like a kelpie out of corsie, clowtie, joup, jimp, limmer, and clobber, and dreiped cantilly – one trusts this is not fatiguing you? – into a sonsie one-piece nichty of sheer tartan flannel. Before popping between the sheets she listened a moment at the door of her bedchamber, into which a careful mother, following the old Argyllshire custom on Hogmanay, had locked her since dusk. From below came a hideous uproar and the crash of breaking glass. Bonnie Mary of Argyll smiled happily. Uncle Hamish's party seemed to be well under way. It was the night of December 31, 1792.

From beneath her pillow the radiant girl, as she snuggled down, drew her new engagement-book for 1793. It seemed to be a pretty kenspeckle New Year from the beginning.

January:    1:  Rin aboot the braes with Mr. R. Burns.
            3:  Gowan-pu'ing (Mr. B.).
            4:  Paidling in the burn (Mr. B.).
            5:  Faulding yowes (Mr. B.).

A louder roaring shook the house as a key turned in the door and kindly, silver-haired Mrs. McBogle entered with a candle. Her daughter greeted her with a merry grimace.

'A' fou?'

'Mumsie, how absolutely braw!' laughed Bonnie Mary, dropping the local patois to some extent. But a graver thought clouded her winsome features almost at once.

'How is that delightful, fascinating Mr. Burns?'

'Ill,' said Mrs. McBogle, lapsing into English likewise. 'Very, very ill.'

Bonnie Mary stifled an exclamation.

'Not so noisily ill,' pursued Mrs. McBogle, shaking her snowy head, 'as your dear Uncle or the Bailie, and by no means in the manic-depressive state of the Procurator-Fiscal and the gentleman with two dirks in each stocking, but very very poorly indeed. In fact, out. Or so I gather from latest reports of stertorous breathing and total collapse behind the sofa.'

Bonnie Mary bit a petulant lip. No brae-rinning with Mr. Burns on New Year's morning obviously. From the distant parlour, during a temporary lull, came an odd moaning or lowing noise, as of a calf in agony. Mrs. McBogle smiled indulgently.

'That,' she said, 'will be the Bailie's English guest, poor Mr. Eric Hopjoy-Hargreaves, who is writing a book on Scottish customs. Unfortunately the British Christmas has already done its work on our Southern friend, who seems to have acute gastric trouble. I never saw a face more drawn, more yellow, an expression more ghastly, more pitiful. Mr. Burns, while he was still conscious, was highly satirical at his expense.'

'They can't take it,' said Bonnie Mary of Argyll in scorn.

'Precisely,' said her mother, moving towards the door, 'the comment of the Laird of Garskadden just before falling under the sideboard about an hour ago. "They canna tak' it, the puir fechterin' Sassenach glowpies", was the Laird's remark – incidentally his last, for he passed a moment afterwards to a better world, like your poor father at Hogmanay 1768. Where is the arnica-bottle? The Bailie has a nasty bruise on his cheekbone.'

'I' the wa' i' the ha',' said Bonnie Mary, relapsing.

Mrs. McBogle understood, nodded and retired, carefully relocking the door.

❄ ❄ ❄

Well, the Laird (whose judgement has ever since been echoed by representative Scottish opinion) was wrong. We think you sahibs *can* take it. So, as a matter of fact, with due reservations, did that eminent Scotsman, Thomas ('Sunny') Carlyle, a great boy for New Year's Eve romps with the Rossettis in smart London restaurants. Carlyle's view that you sahibs can take it was expressed to Cecil Rhodes, with whom he began a long, close friendship at the Magnifique on New Year's Eve, 1878; not, incidentally, as it transpired some time later, the Cecil Rhodes who planned the Cape-to-Cairo Railway, but another Cecil Rhodes, a traveller in linseed, known to the trade as 'Dusty'. On this occasion Carlyle added genially, on being struck with a bottle by a passing sahib in a comic hat and false whiskers:

'Aye! It's magneeficent, but it isna Hogmanay.'

Cecil Rhodes, who had been throwing woolly balls and portions of a cheese soufflé at the Blessed Damozel, paused to beg earnestly for an explanation whereupon Carlyle put his finger unerringly on the essential difference between the true Hogmanay and what passes for it in the South. 'Ye puir gomerals, ye lack *high seriousness*,' said Carlyle.

'Your observations, sir,' remarked a flushed gentleman sitting on the floor close by, 'are at once pertinent and finely expressed. Allow me to shake you by the hand. My name is Walt Whitman.' Another notable friendship was thus born, and though Carlyle discovered in due course that his new friend was not the great American poet but a-from Carshalton of the same name, natural bonhomie always forbade him to allude to this disappointment. Meanwhile his message to the Race still rings down the years. High seriousness is the mark of Hogmanay across the Border, and you sahibs lack it, alas. The fact that 365 days end on December 31 and another 365 begin again on January 1 does not impress you sufficiently with its awful truth. You allow fun and games to interfere with your drinking.

You ask what can be done about this.

The matter was examined in all its bearings at a recent conference of big West End restaurateurs, with a well known managing director in the chair, burying his head in his hands for long intervals and moaning. The difficulty, as the head of Consumer-Psychology-Research pointed out, is that the Race is not happy on New Year's

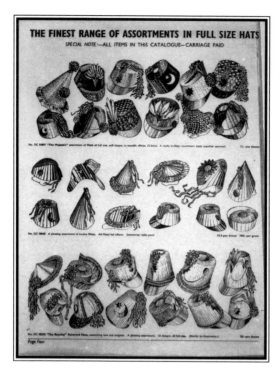

A page from a 1920s catalogue showing party hats.

Eve unless it is allowed to wear comic hats and throw things. The Chairman said hopefully, 'If we held back all the ammunition till Miss Happy New Year comes on with lights-up and the fanfare – but no,' – the chairman, groaning, 'they'd all be asleep except those who were.' After a long silence he added: 'Anybody know anything about Bruce?'

This conversation ensued:

'You mean Izzy Bruce?'

'No, no, no, I mean the Scotch chap. George Bruce or somebody. Didn't he invent some sort of game with spiders?'

(*Long pause*)

'Spiders sir?'

'I was just thinking out loud. What do they *do* all night in Scotland at Hogmanay?'

'Drink I think.'

'And in the intervals?'

'There aren't any intervals.'

A beautiful light shone in every eye, as if everybody saw the fairies, but faded away almost immediately. A wholesale spirit-merchant began to sob like a hurt baby. The Chairman buried his head in his hands again. A hopeless voice said: 'They couldn't take it, anyway. Much too soon after Christmas,' and a woman's musical voice spoke up fearlessly: 'Wilbraham, you wrong our Island heritage!' The Chairman then groaned very miserably and the meeting was over.

# *The Christmas Tree*

## Charles Dickens

I have been looking on, this evening, at a merry company of children assembled round that pretty German toy, a Christmas Tree. The tree was planted in the middle of a great round table, and towered high above their heads. It was brilliantly lighted by a multitude of little tapers; and everywhere sparkled and glittered with bright objects.

There were rosy-cheeked dolls, hiding behind the green leaves; and there were real watches (with movable hands, at least, and an endless capacity of being wound up) dangling from innumerable twigs; there were French-polished tables, chairs, bedsteads, wardrobes, eight-day clocks, and various other articles of domestic furniture (wonderfully made, in tin, at Wolverhampton), perched among the boughs, as it in preparation for some fairy housekeeping; there were jolly, broad-faced little men, much more agreeable in appearance than many real men – and no wonder, for their heads took off, and showed them to be full of sugar-plums; there were fiddles and drums; there were tambourines, books, work-boxes, paint-boxes, sweetmeat boxes, peep-show boxes, and all kinds of boxes; there were trinkets for the elder girls, far brighter than any grown-up gold and jewels; there were baskets and pincushions in all devices; there were guns, swords, and banners; there were witches standing in enchanted rings of pasteboard, to tell fortunes; there were teetotums, humming-tops, needle-cases, pen-wipers, smelling-bottles, conversation-cards, bouquet-holders; real fruit, made artificially dazzling with gold-leaf; imitation apples, pears, and walnuts, crammed with surprises; in short, as a pretty child, before me, delightedly whispered to another pretty child, her bosom friend, 'There was everything, and more.'

The Christmas tree by Brock, *c.* 1900.

This motley collection of odd objects, clustering on the tree like magic fruit, and flashing back the bright looks directed towards it from every side some of the diamond-eyes admiring it were hardly on a level with the table, and a few were languishing in timid wonder on the bosoms of pretty mothers, aunts, and nurses made a lively realisation of the fancies of childhood; and set me thinking how all the trees that grow and all the things that come into existence on the earth, have their wild adornment at that well-remembered time.

Being now at home again, and alone; the only person in the house awake, my thoughts are drawn back, by a fascination which I do not care to resist, to my own childhood. I begin to consider, what do we all remember best upon the branches of the Christmas Tree of our own young Christmas days, by which we climbed to real life.

Straight, in the middle of the room, cramped in the freedom of its growth by no encircling walls or soon-reached ceiling, a shadowy tree arises; and, looking up into the dreamy brightness of its top – for I observe in this tree the singular property that it appears to grow downward towards the earth – I look into my youngest Christmas recollections!

All toys, at first, I find. Up yonder, among the green holly and red berries, is the Tumbler with his hands in his pockets, who wouldn't lie down, but whenever he was put upon the floor, persisted in rolling his fat body about, until he rolled himself still, and brought those lobster eyes of his to bear upon me when I affected to laugh very much, but in my heart of hearts was extremely doubtful of him. Close beside him is that infernal snuff-box, out of which there sprang a demoniacal Counsellor in a black gown, with an obnoxious head of hair, and a red cloth mouth, wide open, who was not to be endured on any terms, but could not be put away either; for he used suddenly, in a highly magnified state, to fly out of Mammoth Snuff-boxes in dreams, when least expected. Nor is the frog with cobbler's wax on his tail, far off; for there was no knowing where he wouldn't jump; and when he flew over the candle, and came upon one's hand with that spotted back – red on a green ground – he was horrible. The cardboard lady in a blue silk skirt, who was stood up against the candlestick to dance, and whom I see on the same branch, was milder, and was beautiful; but I can't say as much for the larger cardboard man, who used to be hung against the wall and pulled by a string; there was a sinister expression in that nose of his; and when he got his legs round his neck (which he very often did), he was ghastly, and not a Creature to be alone with.

When did that dreadful Mask first look at me? Who put it on, and why was I so frightened that the sight of it is an era in my life? It is not a hideous visage in itself; it is even meant to be droll; why then were its solid features so intolerable? Surely not because it hid the wearer's face. An apron would have done as much; and though I should have preferred even the apron away, it would not have been absolutely insupportable like the mask. Was it the immovability of the mask? The doll's face was immovable, but I was not afraid of *her*. Perhaps that fixed and set change coming over a real face, infused into my quickened heart some remote suggestion and dread of the universal change that is to come on every face, and make it still? Nothing reconciled me to it. No drummers, from whom proceeded a melancholy chirping on the turning of a handle; no regiment of soldiers, with a mute band, taken out of a box, and fitted, one by one, upon a stiff and lazy little set of lazy-tongs; no old woman, made of wires and a brown-paper composition, cutting up a pie for two small children; could give me a permanent comfort for a long time. Nor was it any satisfaction to be shown the Mask, and see that it was made of paper, or to have it locked up and be assured that no one wore it. The mere recollection of that fixed face, the mere knowledge of its existence anywhere, was sufficient to awake me in the night all perspiration and horror, with 'O I know it's coming! O the Mask!'

I never wondered what the dear old donkey with the panniers – there he is! was made of, then! His hide was real to the touch, I recollect. And the great black horse with the round red spots all over him – the horse that I could even get upon – I never wondered what had brought him to that strange condition, or thought that such a horse was not commonly seen at Newmarket. The four horses of no colour, next to him, that went into the waggon of cheeses, and could be taken out and stabled under the piano, appear to have bits of fur-tippet for their tails, and other bits for their manes, and to stand on pegs instead of legs, but it was not so when they were brought home for a Christmas present. They were all right, then; neither was their harness unceremoniously nailed into their chests, as appears to be the case now. The tinkling works of the music cart, I *did* find out, to be made of quill toothpicks and wire; and I always thought that little tumbler in his shirt-sleeves, perpetually swarming up one side of a wooden frame, and coming down, head foremost, on the other, rather a weak-minded person though good-natured; but the Jacob's Ladder, next him, made of little squares of red wood, that went flapping and clattering over one another, each developing a different picture, and the whole enlivened by small bells, was a mighty marvel and a great delight.

Ah! The Doll's house! – of which I was not proprietor, but where I visited. I don't admire the Houses of Parliament half so much as that stone-fronted mansion with real glass windows, and doorsteps, and a real balcony, greener than I ever see now, except at watering places; and even they afford but a poor imitation. And though it *did* open all at once, the entire house-front (which was a blow, I admit, as cancelling the fiction of a staircase), it was but to shut it up again, and I could believe. Even open, there were three distinct rooms in it: a sitting-room and bed-room, elegantly furnished, and best of all, a kitchen, with uncommonly soft fire-irons, a plentiful assortment of diminutive utensils – oh, the warming-pan! – and a tin man-cook in profile, who was always going to fry two fish.

What Barmecide justice have I done to the noble feasts wherein the set of wooden platters figured, each with its own peculiar delicacy, as a ham or turkey, glued tight on to it, and garnished with something green, which I recollect as moss! Could all the Temperance Societies of these later days, united, give me such a tea-drinking as I have had through the means of yonder little set of blue crockery, which really would hold liquid (it ran out of the small wooden cask, I recollect, and tasted of matches), and which made tea, nectar. And if the two legs of the ineffectual little sugar-tongs did tumble over one another, and want purpose, like Punch's hands, what does it matter? And if I did once shriek out, as a poisoned child, and strike the fashionable company with consternation, by reason of having drunk a little tea-spoon, inadvertently dissolved in too hot tea, I was never the worse for it, except by a powder!

Upon the next branches of the tree, lower down, hard by the green roller and miniature gardening-tools, how thick the books begin to hang. Thin books, in themselves, at first, but many of them, and with deliciously smooth covers of bright red or green. What fat black letters to begin with! 'A was an archer, and shot at a frog.' Of course he was. He was an apple-pie also, and there he is! He was a good many things in his time, was A, and so were most of his friends, except X, who had so little versatility, that I never knew him to get beyond Xerxes or Xantippe – like Y, who was always confined to a Yacht or a Yew Tree; and Z condemned for ever to be a Zebra or Zany. But, now, the very tree itself changes, and becomes a bean-stalk – the marvellous bean-stalk up which Jack climbed to the Giant's house! And now, those dreadfully interesting, double-headed giants, with their clubs over their shoulders, begin to stride along the boughs in a perfect throng, dragging knights and ladies home for dinner by the hair of their heads. And Jack – how noble, with his sword of sharpness, and his shoes of swiftness! Again those old meditations come upon me as I gaze up at him; and I debate within myself whether there was more than one Jack (which I am loth to believe possible), or only one genuine original admirable Jack, who achieved all the recorded exploits.

Good for Christmas-time is the ruddy colour of the cloak, in which – the tree making a forest of itself for her to trip through, with her basket – Little Red Riding-Hood comes to me one Christmas Eve to give me information of the cruelty and treachery of that dissembling Wolf who ate her grandmother, without making any impression on his appetite, and then ate her, after making that ferocious joke about his teeth. She was my first love. I felt that if I could have married Little Red Riding-Hood, I should have known perfect bliss. But, it was not to be; and there was nothing for it but to look out the Wolf in the Noah's Ark there, and put him late in the procession on the table, as a monster who was to be degraded. O the wonderful Noah's Ark! It was not found seaworthy when put in a washing-tub, and the animals were crammed in at the roof, and needed to have their legs well shaken down before they could be got in, even. There and then, ten to one but they began to tumble out at the door, which was but imperfectly fastened with a wire latch – but what was that against it! Consider the noble fly, a size or two smaller than the elephant: the lady-bird, the butterfly all triumphs of art! Consider the goose, whose feet were so small, and whose balance was so indifferent, that he usually tumbled forward, and knocked down all the animal creation. Consider Noah and his family, like idiotic tobacco-stoppers; and how the leopard stuck to warm little fingers; and how the tails of the larger animals used gradually to resolve themselves into frayed bits of string!

Hush! Again a forest, and somebody up in a tree – not Robin Hood, not Valentine, not the Yellow Dwarf (I have passed him and all Mother Bunch's wonders, without mention), but an Eastern King with a glittering scimitar and turban. By Allah! Two Eastern Kings, for I see another, looking over his shoulder! Down upon the grass, at the tree's foot, lies the full length of a coal-black Giant, stretched asleep, with his head in a lady's lap; and

A Victorian pantomime, R. Seymour, 1836.

near them is a glass box, fastened with four locks of shining steel, in which he keeps the lady prisoner when he is awake. I see the four keys at his girdle now. The lady makes signs to the two kings in the tree, who softly descend. It is the setting-in of the bright Arabian Nights.

Oh, now all common things become uncommon and enchanted to me. All lamps are wonderful; all rings are talismans. Common flower-pots are full of treasure, with a little earth scattered on the top; trees are for Ali Baba to hide in; beefsteaks are to throw down into the Valley of Diamonds, that the precious stones may stick to them, and be carried by the eagles to their nests, whence the traders, with loud cries, will scare them. Tarts are made, according to the recipe of the Vizier's son of Bussorah, who turned pastry cook after he was set down in his drawers at the gate of Damascus; cobblers are all Mustaphas, and in the habit of sewing up people cut into four pieces, to whom they are taken blindfold.

Any iron ring let into stone is the entrance to a cave which only waits for the magician, and the little fire, and the necromancy, that will make the earth shake. All the dates imported come from that same tree as that unlucky date, with whose shell the merchant knocked out the eye of the genie's invisible son. All olives are of the stock of that fresh fruit, concerning which the Commander of the Faithful overheard the boy conduct the fictitious trial of the fraudulent olive merchant; all apples are akin to the apple purchased (with two others) from the Sultan's gardener for three sequins, and which the tall black slave stole from the child. All dogs are associated with the dog, really a transformed man, who jumped upon the baker's counter, and put his paw on the piece of bad money. All rice recalls the rice which the awful lady, who was a ghoule, could only peck by grains, because of her nightly feasts in the burial-place. My very rocking-horse, – there he is, with his nostrils turned completely inside-out, indicative of Blood! – should have a peg in his neck, by virtue thereof to fly away with me, as the wooden horse did with the Prince of Persia, in the sight of all his father's Court.

Yes, on every object that I recognise among those upper branches of my Christmas Tree, I see this fairy light! When I wake in bed, at daybreak, on the cold dark winter mornings, the white snow dimly beheld, outside, through the frost on the window-pane, I hear Dinarzade. 'Sister, sister, if you are yet awake, I pray you finish the history of the Young King of the Black Islands.' Scheherazade replies, 'If my lord the Sultan will suffer me to live another day, sister, I will not only finish that, but tell you a more wonderful story yet.' Then, the gracious Sultan goes out, giving no orders for the execution, and we all three breathe again.

At this height of my tree I begin to see, cowering among the leaves – it may be born of turkey, or of pudding, or mince pie, or of these many fancies, jumbled with Robinson Crusoe on his desert island, Philip Quarll among the monkeys, Sandford and Merton with Mr. Barlow, Mother Bunch, and the Mask – or it may be the result of indigestion, assisted by imagination and over-doctoring – a prodigious nightmare. It is so exceedingly indistinct, that I don't know why it's frightful – but I know it is.

I can only make out that it is an immense array of shapeless things, which appear to be planted on a vast exaggeration of the lazy-tongs that used to bear the toy soldiers, and to be slowly coming close to my eyes, and receding to an immeasurable distance.

When it comes closest, it is worse. In connection with it I descry remembrances of winter nights incredibly long; of being sent early to bed, as a punishment for some small offence, and waking in two hours, with a sensation of having been asleep two nights; of the laden hopelessness of morning ever dawning; and the oppression of a weight of remorse. And now, I see a wonderful row of little lights rise smoothly out of the ground, before a vast green curtain. Now, a bell rings – a magic bell, which still sounds in my ears unlike all other bells – and music plays, amidst a buzz of voices, and a fragrant smell of orange-peel and oil. Anon, the magic bell commands the music to cease, and the great green curtain rolls itself up majestically, and The Play begins! The devoted dog of Montargis avenges the death of his master, foully murdered in the Forest of Bondy; and a humorous Peasant with a red nose and a very little hat, whom I take from this hour forth to my bosom as a friend (I think he was a Waiter or an Hostler at a village Inn, but many years have passed since he and I have met), remarks that the sassigassity of that dog is indeed surprising; and evermore this jocular conceit will live in my remembrance fresh and unfading, over-topping all possible jokes, unto the end of time. Or now, I learn with bitter tears how poor Jane Shore, dressed all in white, and with her brown hair hanging down, went starving through the streets; or how George Barnwell killed the worthiest uncle that ever man had, and was afterwards so sorry for it that he ought to have been let off.

Comes swift to comfort me, the Pantomime – stupendous Phenomenon! – when clowns are shot from loaded mortars into the great chandelier, bright constellation that it is; when Harlequins, covered all over with scales of pure gold, twist and sparkle, like amazing fish; when Pantaloon (whom I deem it no irreverence to compare in my own mind to my grandfather) puts red-hot pokers in his pocket, and cries 'Here's somebody coming!' or taxes the Clown with petty larceny, by saying, 'Now, I sawed you do it!' when Everything is capable, with the greatest ease, of being changed into Anything; and 'Nothing is, but thinking makes it so.' Now too, I perceive my first experience of the dreary sensation – often to return in after-life – of being unable, next day, to get back to the dull settled world; of wanting to live for ever in the bright atmosphere I have quitted; of doting on the little Fairy, with the wand like a celestial Barber's Pole, and pining for a Fairy immortality along with her. Ah, she comes back, in many shapes, as my eye wanders down the branches of my Christmas Tree, and goes as often, and has never yet stayed by me!

Out of this delight springs the toy-theatre, there it is, with its familiar proscenium, and ladies in feathers in the boxes! – and all its attendant occupation with paste and glue, and gum, and water colours, in the getting-up of The Miller and His Men, and Elizabeth, or the Exile of Siberia. In spite of a few besetting accidents and failures (particularly an unreasonable disposition in the respectable Kelmar, and some others, to become faint in the legs, and double up, at exciting points of the drama), a teeming world of fancies so suggestive and all-embracing, that, far below it on my Christmas Tree, I see dark, dirty, real Theatres in the daytime, adorned with these associations as with the freshest garlands of the rarest flowers, and charming me yet.

But hark! The Waits are playing, and they break my childish sleep! What images do I associate with the Christmas music as I see them set forth on the Christmas Tree? Known before all the others, keeping far apart from all the others, they gather round my little bed. An angel, speaking to a group of shepherds in a field; some travellers, with eyes uplifted, following a star; a baby in a manger . . .

# Tales of the Christmas Cracker

## Maria Hubert and Michael Harrison

*In 1982 I was lucky enough to be invited to the Tom Smith Cracker Factory in Norwich. There I was entertained by Mr Varney, who had been an employee when Tom Smith's grandson was there, and he told me all the old tales.*

Tom Smith was a confectioner. Confectioners made sweets, cakes and ice-cream in summer, but the winter trade was always poor. One year, in 1840, Tom and his wife went to France for a holiday. They were very impressed with the French sweets – bon-bons – a hard sweet with a soft centre, wrapped hygienically in waxed paper. At this time in Britain, all sweets were sold loose and unwrapped.

Tom had the idea of bringing the bon-bon to Britain and launching it at Christmas time. To make the sweets even more attrractive he added an outer wrapper, over the waxed paper, on which was written a love motto. These were an instant success, but he realised that within a couple of years, every confectioner would be following his lead. He had to think of something new.

This problem bothered Tom for months, well into the winter season. One day he was sitting by his fire, still thinking, when a log rolled out and lay smouldering on the hearthstone. Tom kicked it back into the flames and it crackled and sparked as he did so. That was it! He would somehow put a 'crack' into the bon-bon. After many experiments his company were able to patent the mercury fulminate 'snap' which was placed in the inner wrapping of the bon-bons. The original bon-bon had in fact been refined by this time – it was now a sweet in a waxed paper, with a motto, then the snap, finished with an outer covering of coloured paper.

Once again, these met with instant success. But with no copyright laws to protect his idea, Tom had to keep one step ahead of his competitors, and within a decade he had invented the cracker, albeit smaller than we know

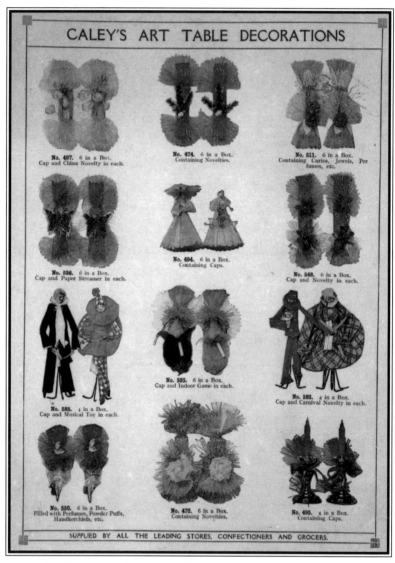

A page detailing nineteenth-century cracker designs by Caley's, who later became part of Tom Smith's company.

it today. It was his son Walter who had the idea of adding a paper hat to the tube, which already contained a toy and motto. By this time competitors were also making crackers. Hovels, who began in a back yard of a terraced house, caused Tom and his company many headaches in the early years. Who could come up with the most innovative, and the most topical, the most beautiful designs? Then Tom Smith got the royal warrant and provided all the crackers for the palace. This put them firmly at the top of their trade, and they were never worried by their competitors after that.

*Michael Harrison, an eminent Christmas historian who wrote in the 1950s, remembers a very special Christmas cracker from his childhood in the late 1920s.*

## Christmas Crackers, the First 100 Years

Christmas without the cracker or (as it used to be called) the 'bon-bon' is as inconceivable as Christmas without the Christmas card; and yet these two essentials to the perfect celebration of Yule were introduced to the world by two Englishmen, only a little more than a hundred years ago: the Christmas card coming, in 1843, three years earlier than the cracker, which was not put on the market until the Christmas of 1846.

Tom Smith, inventor of the cracker. had started work in a confectioner's shop; but when the time came for him to start in business on his own, he resolved to specialize in making the white-and coloured-sugar decorations which are still fashionable for the embellishment of wedding-cakes.

He began to experiment with new patterns, new colours, and – newer still – a higher quality than had formerly been obtainable. On a trip to Paris in 1844 he first saw the then newly introduced 'bon-bon', a packet of sugar plums opened by pulling and thus breaking the wrapping, and was duly impressed with the money-making possibilities of the novelty.

A few weeks before Christmas 1844, Tom Smith, having laid in a stock of fancy papers and sugar-almonds, put his assistants to work wrapping 'bon-bons', which sold well, though the sale slackened off to nothing as soon as the Christmas season had passed.

It soon came to him that he would have to add some further refinement and he conceived the notion of combining the cracker with the Valentine – and so, by 14 February 1843, Tom Smith's 'First Improved Bon-Bon' was ready for the market: the original 'bon-bon' with a romantically affectionate message inside. The motto was born!

The 'bon-bon' soon joined that select company of Christmas necessities: the Christmas tree, the Christmas card and the Christmas-pudding. It was not, however, until 1846 that Smith, by adding the 'bang' – or, as it is called in the cracker-trade, the 'snap' – invented the cracker that we know.

Even with the 'snap', the original 'bon-bon' had not quite become the modern cracker: there still remained the substitution of a 'surprise' for sweets, and the addition of the paper hat. It was Tom Smith who introduced the element of the unexpected into cracker-pulling by putting a small present inside the wrapping, instead of the original handful of sweets – hence the technical term, 'surprise' – but it was Tom's son, Walter, who showed that he had inherited the Smith blood when he proposed to include a paper hat in each cracker.

The paper hat, though, came after a dispensable but still integral part of the cracker: the coloured label.

For the first few years after his invention of the cracker, Tom Smith turned out only one model; but that splendid variety which now characterizes cracker-making all over the world was forced on the inventor by the unheralded dumping of several different kinds of crackers from abroad. With only a few days to go to Christmas, Tom Smith set to by designing no fewer than eight different kinds of wrapping, and had the varieties ready for the market by the time that Christmas arrived.

Victorian cracker-labels are always very plain compared with some of the cards; for the elaboration of the cracker, corresponding to the elaboration of the card, was confined to the wrapper – and here all the ostentation of the secure later nineteenth century could let itself go. There was a limit to the elaboration of the Christmas card: there was technically no limit to the elaboration of the cracker – for apart from the costliness of the wrapper, you might insert the costliest presents you liked.

Millionaires of that happy period felt themselves free to be as vulgarly ostentatious as they liked in the matter of Christmas crackers, and a childhood memory that I have is of a cracker that a guest had taken home from a Christmas dinner at Mr. Pierpont Morgan's house in

Prince's Gate. The twenty-five years or so during which this splendid cracker had lain in a box had not dimmed the brilliant colouring of its purple and saffron satin; of its handmade violets and lilies-of-the-valley; had not yellowed its hand-made Mechlin lace, or tarnished the golden monogram serving for label. I remember that I fingered this superb piece with a greater wonder after having been told that this – and every other cracker on Mr. Morgan's dinner-table – had contained a 'surprise' costing £100!

The cracker has developed another characteristic that puts it apart from the Christmas card: its topicality. At first, the card was inclined to have a topical flavour, whereas the cracker – before label and motto had been introduced – had no flavour of topicality, even if it had a flavour of novelty.

But as the card began to stereotype itself – at least as regards subjects: religious, sentimental, Olde Englysshe, Olde Dykenzienne, and so on – the manufacturers of crackers began to insist on an up-to-the-minuteness in their label and box design which has on occasions led to some quite astonishing results.

For instance, the printing of the labels and boxes for Batgers' Aerial Scouts' Crackers was put in hand in the autumn of 1903. The design shows Boy Scouts flying tractor monoplanes. Now, the Wright brothers' first flight was made on 17 December 1903, in a pusher biplane, in which the operator was lying flat on his stomach, and not sitting upright in the cockpit, as the Scouts are shown in the Batger designs.

Several times, the leading manufacturers have tested public reaction to a modernizing, an enlivening, of the motto. The public have reacted quickly – and definitely. Leave the Corn Alone! can sum up their reaction. The hoarier the mottoes' jokes; the more familiar the jingling doggerel and unabashedly sententious maxim, the happier the public is to read the motto.

# The Twelfth Cake

## From *The Memoirs of a London Doll*
## Richard Henry Horne

*The Twelfth Cake is an old and noble ancestor of our modern Christmas Cake. Its appearance marked the end of the Christmas season at one last, vigorous party. At some seventeenth-century Court revels the cake itself was the focus of these parties, with huge battlefields built on its sugary surface, which two opposing sides would fight over. Earlier still it was known as the Bean Cake, containing within its fruity depths a bean and a pea, and whoever found these pulses were crowned 'King' and 'Queen' of the festivities for the evening.*

*By Queen Victoria's reign, these cakes were baked by commercial confectioners, and sold to anyone who could afford them. It had also become the custom to buy sugar or even porcelain figures to decorate the cake. By this time many houses boasted a cook who would turn her skills to making Twelfth Cake to her own secret recipe. But for those not quite so adept there was always Mrs Beeton's recipe to fall back on! The most significant activity on Twelfth Night was the party. This*

A Regency engraving showing dancing around the Twelfth Cake.

*often took the form of a masqued or costume ball at which a large cake would be served to all the guests. This old tradition of finding a bean in the great Twelfth Cake which exalted the finder to the role of King for the duration of the party was harmless fun, but by the 1870s matters had got out of control. It was not safe to stand looking in a shop window without risking some street urchin's trick of tying your shoelaces or coat tails together. These urchins also put firecrackers through people's doors and other tricks considered 'unacceptable'! Queen Victoria banned the keeping of Twelfth Night as a result of these pranks.*

*If their beloved queen did not like it, the people would not acknowledge it. Christmas Cake replaced Twelfth Cake, although it was often still decorated with the little ornaments that had been designed for the Twelfth Cake. From nursery rhyme characters and Father Christmas models riding sleighs to political figures such as Disraeli – all were arranged upon the snowy cover of rich almond icing. The following extract gives a wonderful description of the Twelfth Cake in the early nineteenth century. We take up the story where a small boy is trying to sell a left-over cake from his grandfather's shop to the masters of a grand London house, which was preparing for the party on the last day of Christmas. The narrative is told by a prized doll belonging to one of the household children; the child is referred to by the doll as 'my mamma'.*

### Memoirs of a London Doll

The boy, without a moment's hesitation, took the cake and held it out flat on the palm of his hand, balancing it as if to show how heavy it was.

'Sir,' said he, 'this is a Twelfth-cake, of very superior make. If the young lady who sits reading there was only to taste it, she would say so too. It was made by my grandfather himself, who is known to be one of the first makers in all Bishopsgate street: I may say the very first. There is no better in all the world. You see how heavy it is; what a quantity of plums, currants, butter, sugar, and orange and lemon-peel there is in it, besides brandy and carraway comfits. See! What a beautiful frost-work of white sugar there is all over the top and sides. See, too, what characters there are, and made in sugar of all colours! Kings and Queens in their robes, lions and dogs, and Jem Craw, and Swiss cottages in winter, and railway carriages, and girls with tambourines, and a village steeple with a cow looking in at the porch; and all these standing or walking, or dancing upon white sugar, surrounded with curling twists and true lover's knots in pink and green citron, with damson cheese and black currant paste between. You never saw such a cake before, sir, and I'm sure none of your family ever smelt such a cake at all like it. It's quite a nosegay for the Queen Victoria herself; and if you were to buy it at my grandfather's shop you would have to pay fifteen shillings and more for it.' 'Thomas plummy!' said the master, looking very earnestly at the boy; 'Thomas plummy! take the doll, and give me the cake. I only hope it may prove half as good as you say.'

. . . the boy ran laughing out of the shop. At the door he was met by his sister, who had been waiting to receive me in her arms: and they both ran home, the little girl hugging me close to her bosom. That evening little Ellen Plummy begged to go to bed much earlier than usual. She took me with her, and I had the great happiness of passing the whole night in the arms of my first mamma. The next morning, however, was the day before Twelfth-day, and there were so many preparations to be made, and so many things to do in the house, that the pastry-cook required the help of every body who could do anything at all; so he desired Ellen to put me in a box till Twelfth-night was over, because he wanted her to sort small cakes and mix sugar plums of different colours, and pile up sticks of barley sugar, and arrange artificial flowers, and stick bits of holly with red berries into cakes for the upper shelves of his shop window . . . About nine o'clock mamma came and took me out of my box. She had contrived to find time in the course of the day to make, in a very hasty manner, a little night-gown and night-cap for me, which she immediately put on me, and then took me to bed with her as before.

Next morning was Twelfth-day, and I was again placed in the dark box . . . I had just begun to get very sad, when suddenly I heard the sound of little feet tripping over the floor; the lid of my box was opened, and I saw a beautiful fairy standing over me. I was taken out by a pair of soft warm hands, and who should it be but my mamma, dressed all in white, with silver bracelets, and roses in her hair, and a bit of most beautiful violet tinsel stuck upon the breast of her frock! 'Come!' cried she, clasping me in her arms, 'come down stairs with me, you poppet! you shall come with me, Maria, and see Twelfth-night!'

Out of the room she ran with me, and down stairs! The staircase was all lighted with gas! I was going to see Twelfth-night! And I had that instant been christened, and my name was Maria Poppet! . . . She ran straight with me into the very shop itself – the fine front shop with all the Cakes! How shall I describe it? How shall I tell the effect it had upon me? Oh, it is impossible. I fainted away.

When I came to my senses I found that my mamma had placed me upright between two tall round glass jars, one full of glittering barley-sugar sticks twisted, and the other full of large sugar plums of all colours; and I was close behind the counter where she stood to serve. I saw nothing else distinctly, my eyes were so dazzled, and so indeed were all my senses. Amidst a blaze of gas, crowded with immense cakes, the round white sugar island of each being covered with its extraordinary inhabitants, there was the front window in all its glory. . . .

Scenes in eastern countries, with elephants and dromedaries and great palm trees . . . negro people and tigers sitting under orange trees; and scenes in northern countries, where all is snow and frost and tall rocks of ice, and bears walking round broken ships; and scenes in delightful countries, where the weather is so beautiful . . . these and many more things were all upon the tops of the large cakes in the lower part of the window, together with sprigs of holly, oh, so full of bright red berries – and here and there shining blanc-mange and jellies in the shape of baskets of fruit and flowers, and three round glass bowls full of gold and silver fish, who constantly moved round, staring, with their noses pushing against the glass, in imitation of a crowd of children outside the shop window, who were all staring and pushing their noses against the glass in just the same way. There was a shelf which ran across the middle of the window, close to the front, and this was also thick with cakes of the smaller sort, and all covered with Twelfth-night characters, in coloured sugar; but what they were it was impossible to see for the glitter of the beautiful barley-sugar sticks that were piled up in the round glass jars, across and across, and standing between the cakes. There were also cakes on a top shelf, near the top of the window, but here scarcely anything could be seen for the blaze of the gas.

In the shop itself there was continually a crowd coming in to buy cakes and other things, for the counter was also covered with delightful wonders, and the old gentleman pastry-cook and great cake-maker himself walked about the middle of the shop, dressed in his best, with a large red rose in the button-hole of his coat, smiling and rubbing his hands together, and chatting with all the children that came in, and sometimes going to the door and giving a handful of sugar plums to children outside who had no money to buy anything.

# *The Royal Christmases of Queen Victoria*

*No anthology of the British Christmas would be complete without reference to Queen Victoria, whose popularity, together with that of her Prince Consort, Albert, was to revive the flagging Christmas traditions of Britain and the whole Commonwealth.*

*While such customs as the decorated Christmas tree flourished in the royal court of the Hanoverian monarchs of the eighteenth century, their lack of general popularity with the people meant that their customs went unregarded. Britain preferred the old Kissing Bough of England – when they bothered at all, that is. Having suffered a huge setback after the seventeenth century restrictions of the Puritan parliament, British Christmas customs were revived under Charles II. However, many of the customs had lost their old symbolism, and were in grave danger of becoming merely an opportunity for riotous behaviour among the wealthy and poor alike.*

*In 1840 the young Victoria married her German prince. They were very much in love and their romance appealed to their subjects. Everything*

*they did became newsworthy and fashionable – even as far away as the
stylish society of east-coast America. Therefore, when they put up their
Christmas tree with all the gifts under it for their young family, this was
recorded in a famous engraving in the* Illustrated London News *in
1848, and the custom was adopted almost universally.*

*This atmosphere brought about a new wave of interest in the old
Christmas traditions. Learned clergymen spent their free time
researching half-forgotten customs and carols. Cooks learned again
how to make Christmas delicacies, children were told about Father
Christmas, whose wild mumming characteristics were toned down by
the gentler but sterner characteristics of the European St Nicholas,
who would leave them gifts if they were good. Christmas cards and
tree decorations were invented and imported from Germany, and Tom
Smith invented what was to become the most popular Christmas
party novelty – the Christmas cracker. This revival of traditional
Christmas celebrations happened during the early decades of Queen
Victoria's reign.*

*The following piece about the royal Christmases comes from a fifty-
year-old copy of* Tatler *magazine, and is presented here with kind
permission of her majesty Queen Elizabeth II.*

## *1840*

On 10 February 1840, Queen Victoria had married her
'dear Albert'. She had married almost in haste – but there
was to be no repentance in post-marital leisure. Victoria
had truly fallen in love at first sight, but as this girlish,
romantic love gave place, in the natural order of things,
to the quieter affection of the long-married wife, no
disillusionment came to cause Victoria the least regret
that she had given her heart completely to her husband.

Now, as the first Christmas of their married life approached, the young couple – she was only twenty-one; he a year older – were drawn even closer to each other by reason of the Queen's pregnancy.

No two people could have been, in the popular phrase, 'more suited to each other'. Both loved the warm intimacy of simple domesticity – 'When,' the Prince once wrote to the Dowager Duchess of Coburg, 'we are not surrounded by a Court and its formalities, our life is so quiet and simple, that it would not fatigue you.'

Albert was a singularly kindly – as well as a kind – man; perhaps we shall get near a true conception of his charm when we say that he was essentially a 'fatherly' man. He was the sort of man to whom little children feel an instinctive need to run – into whose hand they feel the need fearlessly and happily to put their own.

Patient, gentle, tolerant, earnest, simple and good, 'dear Albert' showed a single-mindedness, in the pursuit of love, which marked him as a man of intelligence as well. Other men have striven for fame, for power, for wealth. Albert strove to be loved. Within the narrow limits of the home, he succeeded beyond all measure.

So the young wife drew near to the time of her confinement, and the husband sought to mitigate the natural terrors of the crisis. No one could have been more gentle: a woman – a potential or actual mother – could not have been more understanding of the frets and pangs of expectant maternity.

The queen's first child was born on November 21, 1840. It was a girl – and Sir Theodore Martin records the 'momentary disappointment' shown by the young mother on learning that her first-born was not a boy. But he quickly adds that the disappointment was gone as soon as felt, and that both the parents knew themselves the closer in their joy at having a living token of their love.

Stockmar, the guide (and some have even called him the Svengali) of the Prince, wrote immediately:

'My dear Prince . . . suffer me to remind you, that sleep, stillness, rest exclusion of many people from her room are just now the all-in-all for the Queen.' Albert did not need this advice. Besides he had his own methods of restoring his beloved wife to health. He refused to move from her side: he declined to go to the theatre of which he was very fond until Victoria should be well enough again to go with him.

His infinitely tender care served its purpose well. Long before Christmas the Queen had left her first child-bed and was eagerly making preparations to celebrate the Feast that both she and her husband loved so well.

They left for Windsor.

'All was happiness there. The war cloud had passed away, which for many months had loomed on the horizon, and the dear delights of home had been made more precious by young life which gave it a new and tenderer charm.'

'And as for their first Christmas together, "Christmas", Sir Theodore Martin recalled, "was the favourite festival of the Prince who clung to the kindly customs of his native country which makes it a day for the interchange of gifts, as marks of affection and goodwill."' The Queen fully shared his feelings in this respect and the same usage was then introduced into their home, and was ever afterwards continued [Stockmar], 'Christmas trees were set up in the Queen and Prince's rooms, besides which were placed the gifts with which each took pleasure in surprising the other, while similar trees were set up in another room with the gifts for the household.'

Opening the Christmas gifts, an engraving, 1860s.

They were not all expensive, these gifts 'with which each took pleasure in surprising the other' [Stockmar]. One was an etching that the Queen made of Hayter's portrait of the Prince. And among other trifles, Albert gave his Vicky a little red morocco needlecase. They were to have many Christmases together, but they probably never had a happier Christmas than this, the first of married life. 'Albert brought in dearest little Pussy a sweet white merino dress, trimmed with blue which Mama [i.e. the Duchess of Kent] had given her, and a pretty cap, and placed her on my bed, seating himself next to her. And she was very dear and good. And as my invaluable Albert sat there, and our little love between us, I felt quite moved with happiness and gratitude to God' [Victoria's diary].

They were all at Windsor with old friends such as the Duke of Wellington and Ernst of Leiningen from December 6.

The Prince played often on the organ now he had some songs of his own composition with which to delight their guests. 'Pretty Baby,' to the words of Lord Fordwich, *Kranke Mädchen*, to Reineck's words, and a fine setting of the Anthem, *Out Of The Deep* from Psalms CXXX, vv. 1, 2, 3, 4, and 6.

Best of all the company loved to sing the chorus to the Prince's *Reiterlied*, for which his brother, Prince Ernest of Saxe-Coburg and Gotha, had written the words.

The Queen wrote to King Leopold on December 14.

'We must all have trials and vexations; but if one's home is happy, then the rest is comparatively nothing. I assure you, dear Uncle, that no one feels this more than I do.' And home was, indeed, happy in that magic Christmas of nearly 120 years ago.

### 1861

Christmas was always Christmas with the Queen and her family; but the approaching Christmas of 1861 was to be a Christmas of a special – of a unique kind. Earlier in the year Victoria and Albert had celebrated the twenty-first anniversary of their marriage, and now – as the year drew to its end – preparations were being made to celebrate 'dear Pussy's' [Princess Victoria's] twenty-first birthday. This beautiful, talented eldest daughter – the first pledge of her parents' happiest of marriages – had grown up to be an accomplished artist and musician as well as a young woman of pleasing normal gifts.

'Bertie' was up at Cambridge, and though the Queen and her husband had known the sorrow of bereavement, the remaining Royal children were healthy in body as in mind.

Looking back over the twenty-one years of her marriage, the Queen could only repeat to herself the sentiment that she had expressed in writing to Uncle Leopold at the very beginning of her married life:

'We must all have trials and vexations; but if one's home is happy, then the rest is comparatively nothing.'

Alas! there was a trouble in store for Victoria which was not to be put resolutely aside, since it was a trouble which was to strike at the fundamental happiness, not only of her home, but of the whole pattern of her existence.

The Prince's conscious devotion to what he conceived to be his duty had not been given without cost to him. A man less hardworking than he had been would have felt himself – at a little over forty – to have been hardly out of 'youth', but the Prince knew well that he had prematurely aged himself, and (though he always carried himself with that cheerfulness which is the highest expression of the charm from which it springs) knew that he had exhausted the reserves of his strength.

The Castle was already full of the guests who had assembled for Christmas, among them the Grand Duke and Grand Duchess Constantine, the Duke of Cambridge, Earl and Countess Russell, Lord and Lady Sydney Baron and Baroness Brunow, when the Prince fell ill.

Early in the summer, it had been remarked how tired and worn – almost haggard – the Prince had been looking; but he had refused all suggestions that he should curtail his list of engagements.

In spite of 'not feeling too well' – '*ich bin recht elend*' – 'I feel very done up,' he remarked to the Queen – he insisted on going down to Sandhurst, to inspect the new buildings for the Staff College and the Royal Military Academy. It was the day following 'dear Pussy's' birthday, and afterwards the Prince told the Queen of the '*enissetzlicher Regen*' – the terrific rain – which had greeted the visiting party at Sandhurst, and which had soaked him to the skin. He returned to Windsor by two o'clock, complaining of 'being tired'.

On the day following – November 23 – he seemed better, and went shooting, for several hours, with Prince Ernst of Leiningen. On his return to Windsor, he was greeted with the news of the King of Portugal's death.

The next day he walked to the Duchess of Kent's mausoleum at Frogmore, with the Queen and the royal children, and on the following day insisted on visiting the Prince of Wales at Maddingley. On 28 November, came the thunderbolt of the Trent Affair.

Captain Wilkes, of the Federal American warship *San Jacinto*, had fired across the bows of a British ship, *Trent*. When *Trent*'s captain had hove-to, Wilkes had come aboard with a party and had removed two passengers: Messrs. Mason and Sidell, the accredited diplomatic envoys of the Confederate States to Britain and France respectively. Upon which the Prime Minister's first act – and a most popular one it was – was to order the immediate dispatch of eight thousand troops to Canada.

Of all the men in high positions in Britain at that time, perhaps only one saw the Trent Affair in its true importance – not as an 'affront to British dignity', nor even as 'an outrage on international law' – but as a threat to Anglo-American unity. Most Britons had a sentimental sympathy with the South: the Prince saw that it was not only inevitable, but desirable, that the North should win – for it was necessary to the peace of the world that the Union should survive. He saw what too few people saw with him: that the North–South conflict was not one for the suppression or continuation of slavery, but for the suppression or the continuation of the Union.

The Prince summoned up his remaining strength, and demanded that he see the draft of the Note to be sent to the Federal Government.

The corrections, in the Prince's own hand, are in a shaky script but there is nothing wavering or faltering in the judgement which guided those corrections. Had the Note been sent as originally drafted, there would have been war. By 'toning down' the Note – and saving Federal 'face' – Albert prevented the greatest of all world tragedies: an Anglo-American enmity.

Christmas was coming: the Feast of the Prince of Peace. With his last strength, Albert the Good had stopped a war. . . . He collapsed – his task done. 'I found him lying on the bed in the Blue Room. For days he lingered on, now falling into a coma, now rallying to a charming, touching cheerfulness or dropping momentarily into a resigned sadness – '*Das reicht hin*' (Enough!) he once sighed, his eyes full of tears' [Victoria's diary].

His daughter Alice had the piano moved into the adjoining room, and amid the Christmas decorations going up, she played her dying father his favourite tunes, among them the heart-strengthening assurance: *Ein' feste Burg ist unser Gott.*

'*Liebes Frauchen*' – 'dear little wife' – he called his Victoria. '"*Gutes Frauchen*" he said, and kissed me; and then gave a sort of piteous moan, not of pain, but as if he felt that he was leaving me . . . he seemed to wander and doze . . .' [Victoria's diary].

He was, indeed, leaving her. Leaving all. He died on December 14, and a Society journal of the time carried this item in its next issue:

HAUT TON

On Thursday week, at noon, the Queen left Windsor in the strictest privacy. No person was on the platform at the Windsor station but Lord A. Paget, not even a royal servant was in attendance. The Queen had already adopted mourning clothes, including the widow's cap. As her majesty will be secluded as possible whilst at Osborne more than half of the usual number of Royal servants have been sent to Buckingham Palace.

The journal added:

Dr. Jenner remains at Osborne in attendance upon Her Majesty.

The forty year agony had begun.

## 1899

A hard, bitter winter; with hard, bitter news coming in. The Modder River disaster had shaken something more than the complacency of the British people – it had shaken the world's trust in the 'invincibility' of the great British Empire.

The casualties in the Modder River defeat had made disaster a personal affair for the whole British people – the Queen not least among them. Great names as well as humble had been among the killed. General Wauchope and the Marquess of Winchester had fallen alongside of the rank and file. Remembering another bereaved woman, the Queen, accompanied by Princess Henry of Battenberg and the Duchess of Albany, drove over to Farnborough, on Christmas Day, to visit the Empress Eugenie, whose son had been killed, as a British officer, at Isandhlwana, twenty years before.

On 'Pussy's' birthday, the Prince of Wales had driven to Waterloo to see Lord Roberts off to South Africa. 'Fighting Mac' – Hector Macdonald, had gone by the same boat, to replace General Wauchope as commander of the Highland Brigade. They were difficult days for the Queen.

There was but one more Christmas for her – and she was aware that she had not long to wait to rejoin 'dear dear Albert'.

He had gone on ahead, but he had left much behind. All the courage that she had shown in the forty years of loneliness owed much to his high example. She had not let disaster break her, any more than (she knew) it would have broken him.

She remembered him. She recalled he had loved the simple folk – the common people. Had worked for them, to improve their lot. Much of what is now accepted 'Socialist' legislation owes itself to the Prince's liberal ideas.

'So, on Boxing Day, 1899, the Queen entertained some unusual guests.

'In the afternoon, Her Majesty gave a tea party to which many of the wives and families of the soldiers serving in South Africa were invited. The entertainment took place in St. George's Hall. The Christmas tree stood at the east end and nearly reached the ceiling. The ornamentation of the tree was undertaken by several of the Princesses . . . who superintended the arrangement of the bon-bons, sweets and toys.

'The Queen, after seeing the women and children seated, left the hall for a time, and returning, was wheeled round the tables by her attendants, occasionally speaking a few words to the visitors. The Queen was assisted in the distribution of the Christmas tree gifts by several of the Princesses, and remained in the hall till the close of the entertainment.'

She had seen all the faces of Christmas now. In the very darkening of the shadows, she knew that all the faces were the same. And that all were radiant with the ineffable light of enduring love.

# The Christmas Tree at Windsor Castle

## From the *Illustrated London News*

The Christmas Tree represented in the above Engraving is that which is annually prepared by her Majesty's command for the Royal children. Similar trees are arranged in other apartments of the Castle for her Majesty, his Royal Highness Prince Albert, her Royal Highness the Duchess of Kent, and the Royal household. The tree employed for this festive purpose is a young fir about eight feet high, and has six tiers of branches. On each tier, or branch, are arranged a dozen wax tapers. Pendent from the branches are elegant trays, baskets, *bonbonnières*, and other receptacles for sweetmeats, of the most varied and expensive kind; and of all forms, colours, and degrees of beauty. Fancy cakes, gilt gingerbread and eggs filled with sweetmeats, are also suspended by variously-coloured ribbons from the branches. The tree, which stands upon a table covered with white damask, is supported at the root by piles of sweets of a larger kind, and by toys and dolls of all descriptions, suited to the youthful fancy, and to the several ages of the interesting scions of Royalty for whose gratification they are displayed. The name of each recipient is affixed to the doll, bonbon, or other present intended for it, so that no difference of opinion

Queen Victoria, Prince Albert and the royal Christmas tree, 1848.

in the choice of dainties may arise to disturb the equanimity of the illustrious juveniles. On the summit of the tree stands the small figure of an angel, with outstretched wings, holding in each hand a wreath. Those trees are objects of much interest to all visitors at the Castle, from Christmas Eve, when they are first set up, until Twelfth Night, when they are finally removed. During this period two trees of similar magnitude and general design stand on the sideboard of the Royal Dining-room, and present a brilliant appearance when all the tapers are lighted up, among the branches. These trees are not accessible to the curiosity of the public; but her Majesty's visitors accompany the Queen from room to room to inspect them when they are illuminated. Her Majesty's tree is furnished by his Royal Highness Prince Albert, whilst that of the Prince is furnished according to the taste of her Majesty. The other trees are jointly provided by her Majesty and the Prince, who plan and arrange the gifts on the table. The trees are constructed and arranged by Mr. Mawditt, the Queen's confectioner.

# Mrs Beeton's Christmas Cake

## From *Mrs Beeton's Book of Household Management*, 1853

### Christmas Cake

*Ingredients* – 5 teacupfuls of flour, 1 teacupful of melted butter, 1 teacupful of cream, 1 teacupful of treacle, 1 teacupful of moist sugar, 2 eggs, ½ oz of powdered ginger, ½lb of raisins, 1 teaspoonful of carbonate of soda, 1 tablespoonful of vinegar.

A page from *Mrs Beeton's Book of Household Management* showing seasonal puddings.

*Mode* – Make the butter sufficiently warm to melt it, but do not allow it to oil; put the flour into a basin, add to it the sugar, ginger and raisins, which should be stoned and cut into small pieces. When these dry ingredients are thoroughly mixed, stir in the butter, cream, treacle, and well-whisked eggs, and beat the mixture for a few minutes. Mix the soda with the dry ingredients, being very careful to leave no lumps, and stir the vinegar into the dough. When it is wetted, put the cake into a buttered mould or tin, place it in a moderate oven immediately, and bake it from 1¾ to 2¼ hours.

Average Cost, 1*s.* 6*d.*

# '"Owed" to The Christmas Tree'

## 'A Sharp Old File', 1853

*The Victorian gentleman was not averse to admitting with a great deal of dry humour his feelings regarding the expense of Christmas, even in 1853! There is a popular Victorian Christmas card showing several large billed birds and the motto is 'May all your Bills be little ones'. The following poem '"Owed" to the Christmas Tree' by a 'A Sharp Old File', is in the same vein. A family man recalls the joys of the Christmas tree, which gradually pall as his wallet gets slimmer year by year – quite a perennial theme.*

That Christmas Tree, that Christmas Tree
It is not what it used to be
When I was in my infancy – That Christmas Tree!

That Christmas Tree, that Christmas Tree!
It held its arms out straight to me
With toys in all their brilliancy – That Christmas Tree!

That Christmas Tree, that Christmas Tree!
Aspiring hopes it brought to me!
For King, indeed, I wished to be:
That Christmas Tree!

That Christmas Tree, that Christmas Tree!
My heart leap'd only just to see
The toys that might belong to me
From Christmas Tree!

And happy time, when Christmas Tree
Such stolen kisses promised me,
When I was nearly twenty three.

But now, alas that Christmas Tree
Is sadly changed; indeed to me
'Tis not the same at all to see
That Christmas Tree.

I'm under wed-lock lost the key
I'm fast as any man can be
'Tis called a matter o' money –
As you will see.

Now of the Tree I'm parent stem,
My branches, when I look on them,
My youthful follies I condemn,
As wrong, you see.

My honeymoon had many fees,
In all its lawyer-like degrees,
For then they charge you what they please
Those – never mind.

But when our buds began to grow,
And stood out in an awful row,
And some came out in real full blow
I'd lots to find.

First Tom's commission in the Guards,
And dresses for the girls by yards,
And Joe's false cannons at billiards
Were dreadful blows.

Then suppers that I gave young men
Who never would be off at ten –
Who were so long about the when
They would propose.

The tradesmen flocked at Christmas, too:
Of course, 'they'd got a bill just due,'
For which they must depend on you
To meet at all.

And then the suppers and wax lights
With fiddlers and the harps in flights
And then the men to put to rights,
After each ball.

Then that green brougham, just to show
We were above – all those below;

And let the neighbours see and know
We were genteel.

Next singing, dancing, classics too
Taught me what fathers only knew
In Fortune's wheel.

Then servants with their minds all bent,
Do swelling out what must be spent
With taxes, followers, and rent,
Were awful pests.

Then poor relations in a row,
In their attendance never slow,
Will always patronise you so
And be your guests.

The girls all stick by their mamma,
And sadly sacrifice papa
For boxes at the opera,
Without remorse.

The draper, modiste, wreaths, and gloves,
To decorate my charming doves,
My situation much improves –
'Tis all of course.

Then courting in my house is rife,
And young men will not take a wife
Without a good round sum for life
From out your cash.

Then wedding breakfasts and trousseau
Composed of – what I do not know
Are rather dear parts of the show,
And dreadful trash.

Now these are fatal truths, you see;
And yearly come round all to me
And hang upon my Christmas Tree
Then why should I

Sing praises to a by-gone joke,
Intended for the younger folk?
My merry Christmas is a joke,
To fun defy.

And really 'tis a horrid sneer,
To wish for me a happy year,
When all the wretched bills appear
To tax my purse.

The Christmas 'bills' by Alfred
Crowquill, 1853.

So resolute I still will be,
And say I do not like the tree
That brings such bitter fruit to me
For nothing's worse.

My tree is grand – as grand can be
It brings a prize to all but me
For in each sweet a bill I see
To check my smile
One will stalk in amidst the run
By whom I am that instant done
With rapid bills that always run.

# Christmas Eve at an Old Hertfordshire Farmhouse

## Edmund Hollier

*This account, published in the* Illustrated London News *on Christmas Eve 1853, relates many old seasonal customs and superstitions, and describes Christmas with a gentleman farmer in the early years of the nineteenth century.*

Christmas is a season of boisterous merriment, of hearty physical enjoyment, of feasting and hilarity; but it is also a time of obscure old-world faith and traditionary romance – of poetical beliefs and customs, derived from the superstitions of an earlier day, and lingering, ghost-like, about our winter hearths, even in these utilitarian times. It is true that they no longer form part of our religious creed, and it is well that they do not – for, as matters of serious belief, they are pernicious: yet still they find, and must always keep, a home in every loving and reverent heart, for the sake of their simple, childlike beauty, and for that redeeming sense of spirituality out of which they arose, and which still renders them of interest to all who have any perception of those vast, vague regions which stretch beyond the limits of bare reality.

The only way, however, to see Christmas – and, especially, its advent – surrounded by all its poetical associations, is to spend it in the country. In town it is tricked out in the last new fashions – very pretty to look at, yet in nowise romantic. But there are old, out-of-the-way nooks in England, which, lying from off the great high roads, seem to have been forgotten by the grand reformer, time, and to be the same now as they were centuries ago; places where the dead men, whose very graves have long since vanished from the little, grassy churchyard, might come to life again, and return to their own identical houses, and go back to their work under familiar elms, and find their former haunts and manners still the same. These are the spots where you feel the poetry of Christmas to its full; where you feast, as it were, in the presence of your ancestors, and see in imagination the shades of your English forefathers descend, like a gentle twilight, over all.

I once spent a Christmas after this manner at the house of a friend in Hertfordshire. My friend was a sort of gentleman farmer – a man of education, and passionately fond of ancient customs; and the house in which he lived was one of those delightful old edifices which give you the sense of home more completely than any modern building can. Its solid oaken timbers and massive brick walls did not, perhaps, really exclude the weather more perfectly than the light, economically-built tenements of the present day; but they gave you the *sentiment* of exclusion in a higher degree – and that is much. You seemed fortified – not simply housed – against the assaults of wind and rain and snow. You heard 'the excluded tempest' raving at a distance, and knew that there was more than a brick and a half between yourself

Decorating the house, a Christmas card, 1873.

and it. There was something in the aspect of that old house, as in the aspect of all old houses, which in itself engendered a poetical frame of mind. Who could live for many days among its lustrous-panelled rooms, its deep recessed bow-windows (one of them of stained glass), its fantastic passages leading to strange and shadowy nooks, its legendary chambers, its capacious fire-places, its carved chimney-boards, and its vast echoing flights of stairs, without lapsing into a pleasant dream of antiquity and romance? Who could behold, from outside, its crowding gables and grotesque chimney-pots, – its glowing red-brick wall mantled with ivy, and touched with wandering lines of moss, like gleams of sunlight fixed, without observing to himself, 'This is the kind of nest for a poet to live in'? Who could listen at night to the old primeval language of the wind among the trees with which it was encircled, and not feel a more gentle and awfully loving sense of the Universe come over him?

Another thing which made me like this house better than any other which I had ever seen, was the fact that, although situated in a most woody and rustic part of the country, it was at no very great distance from London; so that its occupants could pass from solitude to the thick of town life, and from that back again to solitude, with little expenditure either of time or trouble. Sitting in a dreamy mood by the fireside at night, one might almost imagine one heard the throbbings of the great heart of the metropolis chiming towards one upon the wind, when it set strongly from the south, this, of course, was merely fanciful, as the place of which I speak is about five-and-twenty miles from London.

One of the plainest signs, at the house of my friend F., of the near approach of the great festival, was the sallying of the whole family into the adjacent woods, accompanied by the men-servants, on the morning of Christmas-eve, for the purpose of cutting branches of evergreen, and of selecting a great log of wood to burn, after the old manger, on the dining-room hearth; for, although F. burnt coals at all other times of the year, he would on no account omit the Christmas yule block. On the occasion to which I am more particularly referring, he entertained us, while we were hacking about the copses, by relating the origin and antiquity of these sylvan tributes to the season. It is true, he observed, that they are of pagan origin; yet they seem to harmonise with the old pastoral character of primitive Christianity, and to be typical of its enduring greenness and its woodland innocence. He reminded us that mistletoe was the sacred plant of the British Druids; and that the old dark forests which, centuries ago, covered the greater part of this island, had often witnessed the solemn processions of white-robed priests through the glooms and the close intertanglements and had seen the mystical branches of this strange parasitical production lopped by golden sickles, and distributed among the people, who would burst forth into the outer daylight, shouting 'The Mistletoe for the New Year!'

He told us that the Celtic and Gothic nations, before their conversion to Christianity, paid equal reverence to this plant; and that even the ancient Greeks regarded it with a religious feeling. He also remarked, on the authority of Stukeley, that the custom of placing mistletoe on the altars of churches was preserved in the North of England even so late as the early part of the last century; and that at York, about the same period, mistletoe was carried on Christmas-eve to the high altar of the cathedral, and a public and universal pardon of all wicked people was proclaimed 'at the gates of the city towards the four quarters of heaven'.

On our return, the yule-log was kindled, and the rooms were decked with the shining branches of evergreens; when my friend straightway grew eloquent

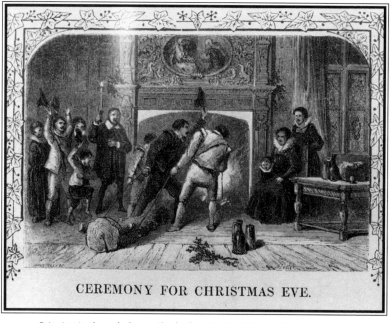

CEREMONY FOR CHRISTMAS EVE.

Bringing in the yule-log in Elizabethan England, Vizelly Brothers, 1840.

on that beautiful superstition about the sylvan spirits
sheltering themselves in these artificial bowers during the
time that their own woodland haunts are cold and dark
and bare. After supper (at which there were mince-pies
enough to give us all indigestion for a year), we had a
huge bowl of wassail – genuine old English wassail; not
made, according to the fashion of some degenerate sons
of their fathers, of foreign wine, but of native ale, just
heightened in its flavour by Eastern spices, and hissing
with a wealth of roasted apples. The greater part of this
having been speedily disposed of; our host proposed that
the remainder should be devoted to a performance which

he said his servants always expected – an old silly custom, as he described it, though I believe he was very well pleased to be a party to its execution – namely, the drinking a health to the apple-trees out in the open orchard.

As we all thought there must be something very picturesque and striking in this ceremony, we were well pleased to be present at it; so, the farm-servants being summoned, away we went to the appointed spot, the oldest of the servants bearing the bowl at the head of the procession.

It was a dark, clear, still night; not cold, and with no falling weather, but filled with that deep solemnity and repose which you can only know to the full in winter and in the country. A sabbath quietness lay over the whole earth, and seemed to stretch upward to the heavens, which, in their vast and starless gloom, appeared hushed into a profound and mighty sleep. The trees and hedges, dimly seen, like intenser darknesses in the more general darkness, gave out no voice, and made no movement; for not the slightest wind was abroad. One of the servants carried a horn lanthorn, which, suddenly revealing in its progress small sections of the landscape, and as quickly merging them into chaos, and every now and then striking up gaunt shadows which lengthened out into the wide vagueness of the night, created around us a sort of phantasmagorical world of advancing and receding shapes. We met no ghosts, however; and, having arrived at the orchard, we formed ourselves into a circle around one of the best-bearing apple-trees (the rogues took good care, in their selection, that no discredit might be attached to the charm, by an untoward result the following autumn), and the wassail-bearer sang, to an ancient tune, that seemed as though it ought have been chanted centuries ago by Saxon tillers of the soil, this stanza:-

> Here's to thee, old apple tree!
> Whence thou may'st bud, and whence thou may'st
>     blow,
> And whence thou may'st bear apples enow!
> Hats full! caps fall!
> Bushel-bushel sacks full,
> And my pockets full too! Huzza!

Here we all set up a great shout, strangely mocked by the echoes; and the old fellow who performed the part of high-priest in this religious observance took a good draught from the wassail-bowl, and threw the rest of the ale, together with the fragments of apple, or 'lamb's-wool', at the tree. We then returned to the house; F. justifying the ceremony by the injunction of Herrick, one of his most favourite poets,

> Wassaile the trees, that they may beare
> You many a plum and many a peare;
> For more or less fruits they will bring
> As you do give them wassailing.

On getting back again to the warm, bright room, another bowl of the same Christmas beverage was brewed; and, in the words of the poet just quoted,

> We still sat up,
> Sphering about the wassail cup.

The yule-log burnt hotly and odorously; the evergreens flashed and flickered in the blaze; the strong liquor steeped our hearts as in the radiance of fifty summers; and we talked over all kinds of delightful Christmas traditions. We spoke of that marvellous old Glastonbury Thorn, which sprung from the staff of Joseph of Arimathea, and from which sprigs have been cut and propagated all over England, and, as the story goes, bud on Christmas-eve, and are in full bloom all the next day until night. We would by no means agree with the modern disbelief in this miracle, which we thought as respectable as many other alleged miracles. We refused to acknowledge that there are similar trees all over the East, from the seeds of which others may be raised in this country; and we execrated the fanaticism of the Puritans, who cut down the original stock during the Civil Wars. From this we passed to graver subjects; and fell to telling the stock ghost-stories of the country round. Thence wider and wider did we launch forth upon the grey sea of Superstition; touching upon remote islands of ghastliness and dread; wandering in grim forests and haunted places between rocks; entering lonely houses upon deserted roads in the evening twilight; lurking about old churches and churchyards 'in the dead waste and middle of the night'; digging for hidden treasure among ancient moss-grown ruins; attending Witch-Sabbaths in solitary barns; straying, in short, over the whole of that wild, dark region of belief which has been finely called 'the night side of Nature'. Not that I, for one, place any serious faith in these dusky mysteries, which, viewed as a creed, can produce none but evil effects; still, while man remains a riddle to himself – while there are such vast, dim, shut-up, chambers in our being – any attempt to people the darkness with tangible forms, however distorted by ignorance or fear, cannot fail to be of interest to all speculative minds, in the absence of certain intelligence. So I have always felt with respect to these matters; and so I believe my friend F. felt.

Among other superstitions of which we spoke, there was one which bears so exclusively upon the Christmas season, that I must here briefly advert to it. It was an old Swedish tradition, to the effect that 'at the festival of Christmas,' according to Olaus Magnus, 'there is a strange mutation of men into wolves, in the cold northern parts; and that these human wolves attack houses, labour to break down the doors, that they may destroy the inmates, and descend into the cellars, where they drink out whole tuns of beer or mead, – leaving the empty barrels heaped one upon another. And one skilled in the manner of this great change of a natural man into a brute, says that it is effected by a man mumbling certain words, and drinking a cup of ale to a man wolf;

and, 'if lie accept the same, the man natural may change himself into the form of a wolf by going into a secret cellar or private wood.'

At length our legends and our wassail came to a close; and, like the party of story-tellers in 'L'Allegro', we retired to bed. Here I had not been long, before I heard the waits singing their carols beneath my window. The music which they chanted was wild, strange, and plaintive, yet soothing; and seemed at once to suggest the idea of 'wind among still woods' at night. I lay in bed listening to them, and thinking at first of the dark, hushed, far-outlying country all about, and of which the voices appeared to be born, the gradually all sense of earth faded from beneath me, and I lay as if cradled in empty space, borne upward by those long, sighing melodies, which seemed as though they had been sounding out of my own heart from all antiquity, and as if they could not cease. They did cease at last, however, and then I fell asleep.

Such were some of the features of the advent of Christmas, as I experienced them at that old Hertfordshire farm-house. Never shall I forget thee, thou pleasant home of comfort and romantic memories and often in day-dreams and night visions, may I behold thy hospitable chimneys rising from out their nestling homestead trees, and walk with thy kind-hearted master (now departed in the body) about thy shadowy corridors and sun-bright rooms, and listen to the voice of thy attendant, woods speaking their eternal secrets to the sky!

# *Windsor Castle Mincemeat*

## The Court Chef, Alexis Soyer, 1861

*The following recipe for mincemeat is said to have been made
at Windsor Castle. It is taken from Alexis Soyer's* Menagerie.
*Alexis Soyer was born in 1809. He only lived for fifty years
but in his short life he became chef to princes, dukes and
marquesses in England and France, and in 1837 became the
Master Chef at the famous Reform Club. In 1838, he created
a coronation breakfast for 2,000, and later went on to
write several books on food preparation and gastronomy.
He also helped Florence Nightingale to reorder the rules of
hospital nutrition.*

The MinceMeat made at Windsor Castle every year, and made
one month previous to using is as follows:

240lb raisins; 400lb currants; 200lb lump sugar;
3lb cinnamon; 3lb nutmeg; 3lb cloves; 3lb ground allspice;
2lb ginger; 300lb beef; 350lb suet; 24 bushels of apples;
240 lemons; 30lb cedrat; 72 bottles brandy; 3lb mace; 60lb
lemon peel; 60lb orange peel.

*I have tried this recipe, turning the pounds to ounces, and then
halving the whole lot; using vegetable suet instead of the real
thing, and adding enough brandy and cider to make a good
mixture. It tastes delicious, and what is left over, properly
sealed down, is even better the following year!*

# 'Winter Sports'

## Anon

*This poem appeared in the* Little Folks Magazine, *Christmas 1877.
It gives a good idea of the sort of snow sports and indoor games
children played, from a snowball fight to the old game of
Snapdragon.*

Jim and Joe, away they go
To build a castle of the snow;
Snow so white the castle walls,
Snow so hard the cannon balls;
And peeping out above the hold,
A giant's head of snow so cold.
'Hallo!' said Jim, 'when all is ready,
And tower and turret made quite steady,
We'll hoist a flag of colours bright,
And then we'll have a jolly fight,
We'll call the castle Giants Fort,
And get our friends to
join the sport.
Hugh, Nigel, Tom, my soldiers three,
To keep the Giant's Fort with me:
Whilst Ambrose, Nugent, little Ben,
Walter, and Charles shall be your men.
And little Bess in scarlet coat,
With comforter about her throat,

Christmas snow sports, a Victorian engraving from *Little Folks* magazine.

Shall be our Queen, and knight us when
We've shown that we are valiant men;
Walter shall bring her, and will see
That she shall safe from danger be.
But now our plans. First, you attack,
And we shall fight, and drive you back;
A battle fought without a blow,
Our only weapons balls of snow.

To take the giant's head your aim;
Whilst to prevent it is our game.
To work! for well on either side,
The troops with balls must be supplied'
Said Joe, 'It is a glorious plan.
I'll work as hard as e'er I can;
And when the battle's fought and won,
We in the house will have some fun
We'll ask the boys all home to tea,
And mother and the girls there'll be;
At Blindman's Buff we'll play, and Post,
And have of riddles quite a host;
And then we'll have, to crown the whole,
Snap-dragon in a blazing bowl,
And as we for the raisins dip,
On fire will seem each finger tip;
Our faces will turn blue, and we
Fire-eaters can pretend to be.
I know that mother will agree;
Our happiness she likes to see.
She says if we our lessons learn,
Some pleasure we deserve to earn,
And as we've worked and prizes won,
She's sure to help us in our fun.'
Ah! winter is as full of joy
To every merry girl and boy,
As is the brighter summer day,
When they can in the meadow play;
Each season brings its own delight,
Or flowers so gay, or snow so white.

# The Mummers

## From Thomas Hardy's
## *The Return of the Native*

*The mummers were a very important part of old Christmas,*
*and indeed still exist in some parts of the British Isles today.*
*In this chapter from* Return of the Native, *the visit of*
*the village mummers is picturesquely*
*described.*

For mummers and mumming Eustacia had the greatest
contempt. The mummers themselves were not afflicted
with any such feeling for their art, though at the same
time they were not enthusiastic. A traditional pastime is
to be distinguished from a mere revival in no more
striking feature than in this, that while in the revival all is
excitement and fervour, the survival is carried on with a
stolidity and absence of stir which sets one wondering
why a thing that is done so perfunctorily should be kept
up at all. Like Balaam and other unwilling prophets, the
agents seem moved by an inner compulsion to say and
do their allotted parts whether they will or no. This
unweeting manner of performance is the true ring by
which, in this refurbishing age, a fossilized survival may
be known from a spurious reproduction.

The piece was the well-known play of 'Saint George',
and all who were behind the scenes assisted in the

George and the Turkish Knight, the Mummers play, by Alfred Crowquill, 1850.

preparations, including the women of each household. Without the co-operation of sisters and sweethearts the dresses were likely to be a failure; but on the other hand, this class of assistance was not without its drawbacks. The girls could never be brought to respect tradition in designing and decorating the armour; they insisted on attaching loops and bows of silk and velvet in any situation pleasing to their taste. Gorget, gusset, bassinet, curicass, gauntlet, sleeve, all alike in the view of these feminine eyes were practicable spaces whereon to sew scraps of fluttering colour.

. . . The result was that in the end the Valiant Soldier, of the Christian army, was distinguished by no peculiarity of accoutrement from the Turkish Knight; and what was worse, on a casual view Saint George himself might be mistaken for his deadly enemy, the Saracen. The guisers themselves, though inwardly regretting this confusion of persons, could not afford to offend those by whose assistance they so largely profited, and the innovations were allowed to stand.

There was, it is true, a limit to this tendency to uniformity. The Leech or Doctor preserved his character intact: his darker habiliments, peculiar hat, and the bottle of physic slung under his arm, could never be mistaken. And the same might be said of the conventional figure of Father Christmas, with his gigantic club, an older man, who accompanied the band as general protector in long night journeys from parish to parish, and was bearer of the purse.

Seven o'clock, the hour of the rehearsal, came round, and in a short time Eustacia could hear voices in the fuel house. . . . Timothy Fairway, who leant against the wall and prompted the boys from memory, interspersing among the set words remarks and anecdotes of the superior days when he and others were the Egdon mummers-elect that these lads were now.

'Well, ye be as well up to it as ever ye will be', he said. 'Not that such mumming would have passed in our time. Harry as the Saracen should strut a bit more, and John needn't holler his inside out. Beyond that perhaps you'll do . . .'

. . . The play was hastily rehearsed, whereupon the other mummers were delighted with the new knight. They extinguished the candles at half-past eight, and set out upon the heath in the direction of Mrs Yeobright's house at Blooms-End. There was a slight hoar-frost that night, and the moon, though not more than half full, threw a spirited and enticing brightness upon the fantastic figures of the mumming band, whose plumes and ribbons rustled in their walk like autumn leaves . . . The house was encrusted with heavy thatchings, which dropped between the upper windows: the front, upon which the moonbeams directly played, had originally been white; but a huge pyracanth now darkened the greater portion.

It became at once evident that the dance was proceeding immediately within the surface of the door, no apartment intervening. The brushing of skirts and elbows, sometimes the bumping of shoulders, could be heard against the very panels.

. . . 'So that we cannot open the door without stopping the dance.' 'That's it. Here we must bide till they have done, for they always bolt the back door after dark'.

'They won't be much longer,' said Father Christmas.

. . . ' 'Tis the last strain, I think,' said Saint George, with his ear to the panel. 'A young man and woman have just swung into this corner, and he's saying to her, "Ah, the pity; 'tis over for us this time, my own."'

'Thank God,' said the Turkish Knight, stamping, and taking from the wall the conventional lance that each of the mummers carried. Her boots being thinner than those of the young men, the hoar had damped her feet and made them cold.

. . . At this moment the fiddles finished off with a screech, and the serpent emitted a last note that nearly lifted the roof. When, from the comparative quiet within, the mummers judged that the dancers had taken their seats, Father Christmas advanced, lifted the latch, and put his head inside the door.

'Ah, the mummers, the mummers!' cried several guests at once. 'Clear a space for the mummers.'

Hump-backed Father Christmas then made a complete entry, swinging his huge club, and in a general way clearing the stage for the actors proper, while he informed the company in smart verse that he was come, welcome or welcome not; concluding his speech with

'Make room, make room, my gallant boys, And give us space to rhyme; We've come to show Saint George's play, Upon this Christmas time.'

The guests were now arranging themselves at one end of the room, the fiddler was mending a string, the serpent player was emptying his mouthpiece, and the play began. First of those outside the Valiant Soldier entered, in the interest of Saint George –

'Here come I, the Valiant Soldier; Slasher is my name;'

and so on. This speech concluded with a challenge to the infidel, at the end of which it was Eustacia's duty to enter as the Turkish Knight. She, with the rest who were not yet on, had hitherto remained in the moonlight which streamed under the porch. With no apparent effort or backwardness she came in, beginning –

'Here come I, Turkish Knight, Who learnt in Turkish land to fight; I'll fight this man with courage bold; If his blood's hot I'll make it cold.'

. . . On the further side of a table bearing candles she could faintly discern faces, and that was all.

Meanwhile Jim Starks as the Valiant Soldier had come forward, and, with a glare upon the Turk, replied –

'If, then, thou art Turkish Knight, Draw out thy sword, and let us fight.'

And fight they did; the issue of the combat being that the Valiant Soldier was slain by a preternaturally inadequate thrust from Eustacia, Jim, in his ardour for genuine histrionic art, coming down like a log upon the stone floor with force enough to dislocate his shoulder. Then after more words from the Turkish Knight, rather too faintly delivered, and statements that he'd fight Saint George and all his crew, Saint George himself magnificently entered with the well-known flourish –

'Here comes I, Saint George, the valiant man,
With naked sword and spear in hand,
Who fought the dragon and brought him to the
    slaughter,
And by this won fair Sabra, the King of Egypt's
    daughter;
What mortal man would dare to stand
Before me with my sword in hand?'

This was the lad who had first recognised Eustacia; and when she now, as the Turk, replied with suitable defiance, and at once began the combat, the young fellow took especial care to use his sword as gently as possible. Being wounded, the Knight fell upon one knee, according to the direction. The Doctor now entered, restored the Knight by giving him a draught from the bottle which he carried, and the fight was again resumed, the Turk sinking by degrees until quite overcome – dying as hard in this venerable drama as he is said to do at the present day.

This gradual sinking to the earth was, in fact, one reason why Eustacia had thought that the part of the Turkish Knight, though not the shortest, would suit her best. A direct fall from upright to horizontal, which was the end of the other fighting characters, was not an elegant or decorous part for a girl. But it was easy to die like a Turk, by a dogged decline.

Eustacia was now among the number of the slain, though not on the floor, for she had managed to sink into a sloping position against the clock-case, so that her head was well elevated. The play proceeded between Saint George, the Saracen, the Doctor, and Father Christmas; and Eustacia, having no more to do, for the first time found leisure to observe the scene around.

. . . The remainder of the play ended: the Saracen's head was cut off, and Saint George stood as victor. Nobody commented, any more than they would have commented on the fact of mushrooms coming in autumn or snowdrops in spring. They took the piece as phlegmatically as did the actors themselves. It was a phase of cheerfulness which was, as a matter of course, to be passed through every Christmas; and there was no more to be said.

They sang the plaintive chant which follows the play, during which all the dead men rise to their feet in a silent and awful manner, like the ghosts of Napoleon's soldiers in the Midnight Review. Afterwards the door opened, and Fairway appeared on the threshold . . . and paused to look along the beam of the ceiling for a nail to hang his hat on; but, finding his accustomed one to be occupied by the mistletoe, and all the nails in the walls to be burdened with bunches of holly, he at last relieved himself of the hat by ticklishly balancing it between the candlebox and the head of the clock-case.

# Cornish Cakes and Other Customs

## From *Christmas in Cornwall Sixty Years Ago*

### Mrs John Bonham

This was the first Christmas that Jenifer and Caroline had been invited to the round of the parties. They were now looked upon as young women, for one was nineteen, and the other nearly eighteen, and both were well grown for their ages. They had already been to eight parties, all at farm-houses, for there were no other homes to which one could be invited. The farmers and their workmen made up the only two classes in the parish, and the latter had not as yet taken to giving parties. At the time Mrs. Olliver and her daughters first consulted together about having a party, the mother thought there would be stout opposition from her husband. When once the die was cast, however, or, in other words, when once she had 'out with it', she would not let it trouble her much. She had informed him of what was coming *off*, and though he might be sulky, she must put up with that.

The morning following the little talk already mentioned, mother and daughters put their heads together as to which day would suit them, and whom they should ask. It was decided that Jenifer should ride round on horseback that afternoon, and give the invitations. So, early after dinner, she set out. There were six farms to call at, and she had to ride quickly from one to another, some being a mile or two apart. All went well, and every invitation was gladly accepted. The sisters in each case were to come in time for tea, their brothers were to follow later on.

The next day Mrs. Olliver began her preparations by making the white bread and saffron cakes. The party was on the following afternoon, and the other cakes and apple pies would be baked then. Soon after dinner on that day, Jenifer, who longed to outshine all others in their spread, consulted with her mother about making some little cakes like those they had seen at the Vicarage tea.

'I'm moost 'fraid to venture,' said Mrs. Olliver, 'cause we aant got no ob'n [oven] to baake little knick-knacks like they. I doon knaw how mutch fire aw'll taake far thom, saame my life.'

'Law, mother, *you* can baake th' orn fast if enough ef you'll *try*. I'll be gone an' maake th' orn, far the cook said to me how they was done.'

So the butter and flour were mixed, and the eggs, sugar, and cream added. The hot baking-iron was well wiped and greased, and bits of the rich mixture dropped on it. Then all was covered with the baker, and Mrs. Olliver began, not without misgivings, to 'blast' the precious little cakes.

'I'm all of aw tremble,' she said, 'far I no moore knaw how much – fire aw'll taake to baake thorn than the dead in the grave.' Jenifer watched her mother eagerly. 'Es that enough, I wonder?' she asked, carefully placing another blazing bush of furze on the baker.

'Why no,' replied Jenifer, 'that'll never sawk [soak] thorn; put bit moore fire, mawther.'

Another bush was added. 'Theere, theere,' said Mrs. Olliver quickly, 'I'm 'fraid of my life to put any more, ar they may be burnt to rags.'

After about twenty minutes they thought it might be well just to have a peep at them. The hot ashes were brushed aside, and Jenifer was to look under while her mother partly lifted the baker. Suddenly the poor girl uttered a bitter yell. 'O-o-oh! my goodness guide ine! they are all so black as aw cawi [coal].'

Mrs. Olliver in her fright let the baker drop down suddenly. 'Never, to be sure,' she cried in great distress.

'Iss they are,' replied Jenifer, ready to burst out crying. The baker was lifted off with trembling hands, when a round, black, charred mass met their eyes. So ended the little cakes, so rich and on which they had bestowed much thought and labour; and thus was foiled a presumptuous attack on the supremacy of 'the Vicarage Tea'.

Caroline was upstairs making that part of the house in perfect order for the visitors, and she was called to sympathise with the sorrowing ones. But there was no time to be lost, for other matters claimed their attention. 'Little cakes,' however, must not be thought of again. Mrs. Olliver, of course, inwardly bewailed the wasted butter and eggs and sugar and cream, but seeing how cut up her daughter was, wisely said nothing. Soon the apple pies were made, and baked to a 'T' by Mrs. Olliver, who could turn out anything to perfection in her own line of baking. As she said herself, when after some days the keen-ness of the disappointment had rubbed off; 'I doon knaw nawthen' 'bout sush fiddlefaddles. We mus' stick to the good ol'-fashen' fare of saffern and heavy cake, and good apple-pie and cream.'

The time wasted over the little cakes had interfered with the progress of the preparations. The strangers were expected before five o'clock, and it was now after three, and still the heavy cakes were not made. Caroline, good creature that she was, having finished her share of the preparations, now worked with real goodwill to help her sister forward, cutting bread-and-butter, assisting in laying the table, also urging her sister to 'get changed', that she might be ready to receive the visitors.

Mrs. Olliver brought out her rare old china that had belonged to her grandmother. The teapot was very large and almost square in shape, and the fiddle-pattern silver spoons shone brilliantly. The table looked well, and though Jenifer still mourned the absence of the little cakes that would have marked their spread as something extraordinary, yet consoled herself with the thought that everything was of the best quality. Milking the cows could not be thought of on such an occasion; so Martha Trezise, who often came to help for an hour or so, was to undertake that for them.

Jenifer in her own anxiety, this being the first young people's party, had not yet seen the way clear to get

A Christmas tea party in a Cornish farmhouse, Vizelly Brothers, 1840.

upstairs to change. This thing worried her, then the other, so that the poor girl was in quite a state of nervous irritability. The three children now arrived from the village school much earlier than usual, for, having found out they were going to have a 'tay' party, they set off for home at full speed, and came rushing in 'like wild things', and immediately planted themselves in the parlour door, lost in wonder at the table and the coal fire – a thing they rarely saw. Jenifer nearly upset a plate of bread-and-butter when they turned round quickly to see who was coming. This was the last straw to break the camel's back. She forgot herself for once, and vented her pent-up feelings on the innocent children. 'Get along weth 'a all this minute,' she cried spitefully, at the same time giving them a rough push, 'or I'll scat 'a maslin. – Mawther,' she called out, 'the cheldurn shaan't come in glazing 'bout the parlour, they nearly maade me arverset the things. They aarn't goon' t'ave tay weth we; they must wait an', 'ave et weth faather.'

'Iss, iss, cheldurn, you mus'n't 'ender the maidens,' called out Mrs. Olliver, with red face and blearing eyes from blasting the heavy cakes. So the three longing, curious children – banished to the kitchen – had to content themselves with a taste of cake till they had their tea with father, for none could induce him to join the strangers.

Jenifer made a hasty toilet, her heart beating violently for fear a knock should come before she was ready, and mother might answer the door in her *déshabillé*. Caroline, too, was not fit to receive company as yet, as she was still busy in the dairy. Poor girls, both busily at work since early morning, what a day they had had!

Snow-covered fields, by Ralph Caldecott, from *Old Christmas, from the Sketch Book of Washington Irving*, 1875.

# 'The Ballade of Christmas Ghosts'

## Andrew Lang

*Andrew Lang was a Scottish author famous for his collections of folk tales and fairy stories, of which he made a lifelong serious study. Between 1872 and his death in 1912, he produced dozens of books on folk-lore, anthropology, ballads, myths and legends. 'The Ballade of Christmas Ghosts' is one of his Christmas ballads.*

Between the moonlight and the fire
In winter twilights long ago
What ghosts we raised for your desire
To make your merry blood run slow!
How old, how grave, how wise we grow!
No Christmas ghost can make us chill,
Save those that troupe in, mournful now,
The ghosts we all can raise at will.

The beasts can talk in barn & byre
On Christmas Eve, old legends know,
As year by year the years retiire,
We men fall silent then, I trow.
Such sights hath memory to show,
Such voices from the silence thrill,
Such shapes return with Christmas snow;
The ghosts we all can raise at will.

Oh, children of the village choir,
Your carols on the midnight throw!
Oh! Bright across the mist and mire
Ye ruddy hearths of Christmas glow!
Beat back the dread, beat down the woe,
Let's cheerily descend the hill;
Be welcome all to come or go,
The ghosts we all can raise at will!

Envoy
Friend, *Sursum Corda*,[1] soon or slow
We part like guests, who've joy'd their fill;
Forget them not, nor mourn them so,
The ghosts we all can raise at will.

# *Reminiscences of Christmas*

## From *Sketches by 'Boz'*
## by Charles Dickens

*I make no apology for including here the almost complete
Christmas sketches from Dickens' writings between 1832 and 1836.
'Boz' was a pseudonym used by Dickens in his essays for the*
Chronicle *newspaper. The 'Sketches' were later published all
together as* Sketches by 'Boz'. *Illustrative of everyday life and*

1. *Sursum corda* – lift up your hearts.

*everyday people'. They are, among all of Dickens' work, largely ignored in favour of his more popular material written in later life. But these short essays, originally produced as a series of magazine articles by the young Dickens, describe a Dickensian Christmas far better, to my mind, than many of his later and more popular stories did.*

Christmas time: That man must be a misanthrope indeed, in whose breast something like a jovial feeling is not roused, in whose mind some pleasant associations are not awakened by the recurrence of Christmas . . . draw your chair nearer the blazing fire – fill the glass and send round the song – and if your room be smaller than it was a dozen years ago, or if your glass be filled with reeking punch, instead of sparkling wine, put a good face on the matter, and empty it off hand, and fill another, and troll off the old ditty you used to sing, and thank God it's no worse. Look on the merry faces of your children (if you have any) as they sit round the fire . . .

Who can be insensible to the outpourings of good feeling, and the honest interchange of affectionate attachment, which abound at this season of the year? A Christmas family-party: We know nothing in nature more delightful; There seems a magic in the very name of Christmas. Petty jealousies and discords are forgotten . . .

The Christmas family-party that we mean, is not a mere assemblage of relations, got up at a week or two's notice, originating this year, having no family precedent in the last, and not likely to be repeated in the next.

No. It is an annual gathering of all the accessible members of the family, young or old, rich or poor; and all the children look forward to it, for two months beforehand, in a fever of anticipation. Formerly, it was held at grandpapa's; but grandpapa getting old, and grandmamma getting old too, and rather infirm, they have given up house-keeping, and domesticated themselves with Uncle George; So that party always takes place at Uncle George's house but grandmamma sends in most of the good things and grandpapa always will toddle down, all the way to Newgate Market to buy the turkey, which he engages a porter to bring home behind him: in triumph, always insisting on the man's being rewarded with a glass of spirits, over and above his hire, to drink 'a merry Christmas and a happy new year' to Aunt George. As to grandmamma, she is very secret and mysterious for two or three days before-hand, but not sufficiently so to prevent rumours getting afloat that she has purchased a beautiful new cap with pink ribbons for each of the servants, together with sundry books and pen-knives, and pencil-cases for the younger branches; to say nothing of divers secret additions to the order originally given by Aunt George at the pastry-cook's, such as another dozen of mince-pies for the dinner, and a large plum-cake for the children.

On Christmas Eve, grandmamma is always in excellent spirits, after employing all the children, during the day, in stoning plums, and all that, insists, regularly every year, on Uncle George coming down into the kitchen, taking off his coat, and stirring the pudding for half an hour or so; which Uncle George good-humouredly does, to the vociferous delight of the children and servants. The evening concludes with a glorious game of blind-man's-buff, in an early stage of which grandpapa takes great care to be caught, in order that he may have an opportunity of displaying his dexterity.

On the following morning, the old couple, with as many of the children as the pew will hold, go to church in great state: leaving Aunt George at home dusting decanters and filling casters [a serving jug], and Uncle George carrying bottles into the dining-parlour, and calling for corkscrews, and getting into everybody's way.

When the church-party return to lunch, grandpapa produces a small sprig of mistletoe from his pocket, and tempts the boys to kiss their little cousins under it – a proceeding which affords both the boys and the old gentleman unlimited satisfaction, but which rather outrages grandmamma's idea of decorum, until grandpapa says that when he was just thirteen years and three months old, he kissed grandmamma under a mistletoe too, on which the children clap their hands, and laugh very heartily, as do Aunt George and Uncle George and grandmamma looks pleased, and says, with a benevolent smile, that grandpapa was an impudent young dog, on which the children laugh very heartily again, and grandpapa more heartily than any of them.

But all these diversions are nothing to the subsequent excitement when grandmamma in a high cap, and slate-coloured silk gown; and grandpapa with a beautifully plaited shirt frill, and white neckerchief; seat themselves on one side of the drawing-room fire, with Uncle George's children and little cousins innumerable, seated in the front, waiting the arrival of the expected visitors. Suddenly a hackney-coach is heard to stop, and Uncle George, who has been looking out of the window exclaims, 'Here's Jane!' on which the children rush to the door, and helter-skelter downstairs; and Uncle Robert and Aunt Jane, and the dear little baby, and the nurse, and the whole party, are ushered upstairs amidst tumultuous shouts of 'Oh, my:'. . .

And when, at last, a stout servant staggers in with a gigantic pudding, with a sprig of holly in the top there is such laughing and shouting, and clapping of little chubby hands, and kicking up of fat dumpy legs, as can only be equalled by the applause with which the astonishing feat of pouring Lighted brandy into mince-pies is received by the younger visitors. Then the dessert: – and the wine: – and the fun: Such beautiful speeches, and such songs.

Next to Christmas-day, the most pleasant annual epoch in existence is the advent of the New Year. There are a lachrymose set of people who usher in the New Year with watching and fasting, as if they were bound to attend as chief mourners at the obsequies of the old one. Now, we cannot but think it a great deal more complimentary, both to the old year that has rolled away, and to the New Year that is just beginning to dawn upon us, to see the old fellow out, and the new one in, with gaiety and glee.

There must have been some few occurrences in the past year to which we can look back, with a smile of cheerful recollection, if not with a feeling of heartfelt thankfulness. And we are bound by every rule of justice and equity to give the New Year credit for being a good one, until he proves himself unworthy of the confidence we repose in him.

This is our view of the matter; and entertaining it, notwithstanding our respect for the old year, one of the few remaining moments of whose existence passes away with every word we write, here we are, seated by our fireside on this last night of the old year, one thousand eight hundred and thirty-six, penning this article with as jovial a face as if nothing extraordinary had happened, or was about to happen, to disturb our good humour.

Hackney-coaches and carriages keep rattling up the street and down the street in rapid succession, conveying, doubtless, smartly-dressed coachfuls to crowded parties; loud and repeated double knocks at the house with green blinds, opposite, announce to the whole neighbourhood that there's one less party in the street at all events; and we saw through the window, and through the fog too, till it grew so thick that we rung for candles, and drew our curtains, pastrycooks' men with green boxes on their heads, and rout-furniture warehouse-carts, with cane seats and French lamps, hurrying to the numerous houses where an annual festival is held in honour of the occasion.

We can fancy one of these parties, we think, as well as if we were duly dress-coated and pumped, and had just been announced at the drawing-room door.

Going to a party, R. Seymour, 1836.

Take the house with the green blinds for instance. We know it is a quadrille party, because we saw some men taking up the front drawing room carpet while we sat at breakfast this morning, and if further evidence be required, and we must tell the truth, we just now saw one of the young ladies 'doing' another of the young ladies' hair, near one of the bedroom windows; in an unusual style of splendour, which nothing else but a quadrille party could possibly justify.

# Candied Walnuts, English Caramels and Preserved Violets

## Recipes for Sweets from *Home Notes*, 1898

*In Victorian England most sweets were still sold unwrapped, so many mothers encouraged their children to make their own sweetmeats at Christmas time for hygienic reasons. The following recipes are from the 1898 Christmas Eve issue of the young ladies' weekly paper,* Home Notes, *under the heading of 'Seasonable and Dainty Cookery'.*

### Candied Walnuts

Procure some nice fresh walnuts, remove the shells, keeping the nut perfectly whole. Take a needle & thread and pierce through the centre of the nut lengthways. Several nuts may be placed on the same thread provided they do not touch. Make a syrup by boiling together one pound of sugar and half a pint of water; let it boil without stirring, until a drop of the syrup will harden directly it is dropped upon a cold plate. Immediately before removing from the fire, add a pinch of Cream of Tartar dissolved in a drop of water.

Now dip the stringed nuts into the syrup for a few seconds, and then hang them in a cool place where they do not touch anything. If more than one nut is on the thread a deeper pan will be necessary for the syrup. When dry keep in tins in perfectly dry conditions.

**English Caramels**

Two ounces of grated chocolate, six ounces of white sugar and a piece of butter the size of a cob nut [about ¾oz]. Place the ingredients in a pan and add to them half a teacupful of hot water and stir until it boils. Let it boil for ten minutes, then drop a little of the mixture in cold water. As soon as it is the consistency of thick treacle, pour it into well buttered tins and stir it about with a silver spoon until it looks glossy. Cut the caramel into short pieces and store in airtight tins.

**Preserved Violets**

Boil a pound of loaf sugar with a small quantity [¼ pint] of water until when dropped on a cold plate it becomes brittle. Have ready some large double violets, free from stalk, and drop them in the syrup a few at a time, leaving them until the syrup comes back to boil. Stir the sugar around the edge until it looks white and grainy, then gently stir the flowers until the sugar parts away from them. Set the violets on a sieve, and place them in a cool oven to dry. Store in airtight tins for future use. You can use this recipe for primroses, mint leaves and rose petals.

[**Author's note:** You will need to practise this last recipe to get the right consistency before wasting petals. I have tried it, and it works beautifully if you use a sugar thermometer and heat the sugar to 'hard crack' – 154 °C/320 °F, I find it best to use a wide shallow pan, so all the flowers can be done at once, otherwise the sugar becomes too brown before the process is completed.]

# 'A Fenland Carol'

## Rudyard Kipling

*This carol, sung by Waits and Carollers at Fenland houses around the turn of the nineteenth century, can be sung to the tune of 'God Rest Ye Merry, Gentlemen'. It was originally part of 'The Tree of Justice' in* Rewards and Fairies, *published in 1910.*

Our Lord who did the Ox command
To kneel to Judah's King,
He binds His frost upon the land
To ripen it for Spring –
To ripen it for Spring, good sirs,
According to His Word.
Which well must be, as ye can see –
And who shall judge the Lord?

When we poor Fenmen skate the ice
Or shiver on the Wold,
We hear the cry of a single tree
That breaks her heart in the cold –
That breaks her heart in the cold, good sirs,
And rendeth by the board,
Which well must be, as ye can see –
And who shall judge the Lord?

Her wood is crazed and little worth
Excepting as to burn,
That we may warm and make our mirth
Until the Spring return –
Until the Spring return, good sirs,
When Christians walk abroad;
Which well must be, as ye can see –
And who shall judge the Lord?

God Bless the Master of this house,
And all who sleep therein!
And guard the Fens from pirate folk,
And keep us all from sin,
To walk in honesty, good sirs,
Of thought and deed and word!
Which shall befriend our latter end –
And who shall judge the Lord?

## 'Christmas Eve'

### Ruth and Celia Duffin

*All over Ireland on Christmas Eve the visitor will see lights in the
windows of the houses – candlelights, lighted trees, modern wooden
candle pyramids, all kinds of lights – but these are not merely decorations.
The practice of illuminating the window is based on the old custom of
putting a light in a window to guide the traveller, which originated from*

'The light in the window' by
Jung Sook Nam.

*days when the rules of hospitality were paramount. On Christmas Eve*
*the light was placed there in remembrance of the Holy Family trudging*
*from one inn to another trying to find shelter. Every Irish home bids*
*them welcome. This poem, 'Christmas Eve', encapsulates the tradition.*

A cup of milk,
A wheaten cake,
And a spark of fire
For the Traveller's sake.

A door on the latch
A light in the pane,
Lest the Travellers pass
In the wind and the rain.

For food, and fire
And candlelight,
The Traveller's blessing
On us this night.

# The Wondrous Tree of Christmas

## Glyn Griffiths

*A childhood memory of celebrating Christmas in a small
Ebenezer chapel community in Wales would not normally inspire
one to write of the event as being 'most memorable'. But in
'The Wondrous Tree of Christmas' Glyn Griffiths manages to
ee the magic of Christmas despite the grim chapel and
its strict elders.*

If you were to ask – and it would be quite futile at this
stage for you not to – what to me represents the
Christmases of childhood, I would without hesitation
(having prepared my answer well beforehand) say the old
chapel on the corner.

The tired box-like edifice, with its grey walls and
rusting gate and the slate slab above the door marked
Salem or Gerizim or Ebenezer or Horeb: the entire
geography of Palestine has been inscribed on these slabs
of Welsh slate. Do you remember it? Of course you do.
You have only to close your eyes and it comes floating
towards you along the screen of the inward eye. You can
call back every feature of its featureless architecture,
recapture every mood that was demonstrated there. Why,
even across the years there comes to you this very
moment the smell of the place – polished pinewood,
Mintoes and the astringent odour of piety.

Yes, there are the remorseless pews facing a remorseless pulpit which has taken up a defensive position in the framework of the deacons' seat. There is the door to the vestry, which creaks, there are the opaque windows where bluebottles buzz on long summer Sundays. And there's the clock in the gallery.

If there is anything about the chapel that you will remember, it will be that clock. It's the slowest moving timepiece in creation – as slow as the mills of God. The clock at home devours the hours; this one takes a small eternity to move from one moment to the next. And if the sermon is more tedious than usual, it slows down almost to a stop.

What aeons of time you have wasted peering over the edge of the pew at that obtuse clock, calculating the possible moment of your release from captivity. And as you have grown older, haven't you wished that all the clocks in the world would ease up and settle to the gradual pace of the clock in the gallery of the old chapel at home?

But on Christmas night there was a transformation. Even the clock perked up and went rattling along at a fair lick. The usual bareness of the interior would be softened, too. The deacons, normally dedicated to the principle that a stained glass window was an abomination in the eyes of God and that any adornment was an eighth deadly sin would, guiltily perhaps (as the Israelites were with the Golden Calf as soon as Moses had gone mountaineering), gild and garnish the old edifice until it twinkled and shone with the self-consciousness of a middle-aged spinster at a youth dance.

The pulpit, seat of denunciation against the vain pomps of a visible world, would be temporarily bound, gagged and hidden by a tide of greenery, pricked here and there with the blood-drops of berry; the satined holly leaves would glint wicked and Babylonian in the light of the blue gas jets.

The deacons' arena, where normally the elders deposited their grave and enduring bottoms, would take on the aspect of a pagan arbour out of which rose (oh! unutterable majesty) the tallest, fattest, most wondrous Christmas tree, whose beauty just stopped short of being downright sinful. And its branches bore the richest argosy of gifts in the world.

I couldn't begin to tell you what was there to dazzle the mind, seduce the eye and tempt the soul: combs in celluloid cases, handkerchieves too small and dainty for any mortal nose; strawfilled dolls from the sixpenny shop, turkish delight, scarves and figs, penknives, golliwogs, hairbrushes, tins of brilliantine of violent lavender, packets of seeds that when placed in water would erupt into a tangle of wet paper which was supposed to represent Japanese flowers, tea caddies with the picture of Edward VII (very wicked, God forgive him), policemens' hats and crackers, whistles, licorice sticks, improving literature, button-hooks and clockwork cars, games of rash chance like ludo and snakes and ladders.

Each gift has a number on it. This number corresponds to the number printed on your ticket. One of those gifts is yours. Which one? Steady on there. Damp down the flame of anticipation. Remember the painful anti-climax of other years. Remember the box of lead soldiers you coveted the year you got a copy of an edifying volume called *The Canal boy who became President*. So edifying that you've never read it. But it's not easy to fill that large tremulous hole that has materialised in your stomach as the long pole with the hook searches among those branches and you await the calling of your number. Oh! The terror, the tension. Oh! The ecstasy of it.

When the gifts are all distributed, the branches nude and half the congregation directing envious glances at the other half, why, only part of this immortal Christmas night is over. There's more to come. Much more.

Didn't I tell you that this is the Annual Christmas Tree *and* Concert? Look, it's capitalised thus on the ticket. Now is the far and fierce hour of Mr. Gogwyn Jones. Who more capable than he of assuaging your disappointment in song and merriment? What use to laud your Beechams, your Toscaninis and your Sargents to a man who has known the full glory of Mr. Gogwyn Jones.

Don't toss me that tale of the irascibility of Beecham. When did he ever have the courage to stop a choir in full throat at a public entertainment and tersely inform them that they were out of tune? Just you try to tell fifty Welsh quarrymen, known for their phlegm and muscular capacity, to get into tune and start again. Right from the beginning. And you can begin to grasp what kind of man was Mr. Gogwyn Jones.

Your Sargents? Pshaw! When did he ever lay down his baton after a spirited rendering of 'Martyrs in the Arena' and launch into a duet called 'Madam, will you walk'? That's versatility for you. And what of prim buttonholes and sartorial elegance? Did your Sargents ever make a public appearance in a pepper-and-salt suit and spats? That's the kind of Olympian gesture you could expect of Mr. Gogwyn Jones. Spats!

And with what rare talent he served his public. Oh yes, Mr. Gogwyn Jones knew what they wanted. His programmes were invariable; you can never have too much of a good thing. There was 'Crossing the Plain', with those quarrymen challenging the silent Christmas night with their cries of triumph. For years they had cheerfully thundered their way across the trails of that familiar plain. What matter if the tone got a little ragged now and then. Mr. Gogwyn Jones, moist but determined, was in the van to lead a few wandering tenors or a brace of errant basses back from truancy.

There was 'The Shipwreck', a dramatic recitation given by Miss Triphena Jones, compelling of eye and deep of voice who could launch the lifeboat in the direction of the harmonium with a cry of 'into the heaving main the brave ship swiftly sped' so as to make your flesh creep. And if no-one happens to be about, just you try shouting 'the brave ship swiftly sped' at the top of your voice. It takes the subtle genius of Miss Triphena Jones to keep those sibilants dry and under control.

Then would come duets and piano solos and comic dialogues and star appearances of Mrs. Hugo-Vance, who still emitted a whiff of the greatness that once was hers as a member of the chorus of the Carl Rosa Opera Company. She, despite her seventy-three summers, could make a ballad of maidenly love-sickness sound credible. When she sang 'My young love awaits where the roses grow' why, no-one ever conjectured as to the inordinate length of his wait and the longevity of those roses.

Down the dusty corridor of the wasted, disillusioned years I catch even now the faint echo of her voice, standing there surrounded by the ivy and the holly (now wilting steadily), her painted cheeks with a flicker of gas light on them, her eyes shut and the masses of puce lace she always wore possessed by aspen tremors. 'Jer-oooosalem, Jer-ooos-alem . . . Hos-aaa-nnah hi-i-in the hi-highest'. The thin and now uncertain voice would lift itself through the roof and go wing-ing towards the uncaring stars, lingering there like a promise above the dark-ness of Christmas night, a promise that some-how I still hope is going to be kept.

An illustration of a Christmas tree from a magazine, *c.* 1900.

# Village Christmas

## Cyril Palmer

*In the early postwar years rural Christmases were very different*
*from town Christmases. With the sophistication of the 1960s*
*still far off, village people observed the same customs that their*
*villages had done for centuries. Moving to a village from*
*London was a major cultural shock and the following*
*account is by a London 'townie' who made*
*just such a move.*

Christmas that year was all quite different. We had recently moved from a London suburb to our home in the country – a small village which the whole family took to their hearts the moment they saw it – and we felt that the celebration of Christmas would also be an excellent way of celebrating the end of our settling in period. And so it proved.

The first real sign of our approaching village Christmas was the delivery of the Christmas tree. It arrived at the weekend, so that gave us a good opportunity to take a pre-arranged stroll to gather branches of holly to augment our own supply of garden greenery for decorating the house. The next day, Sunday, was hectic, although Christmas was still a whole week away. Like so many other families, on the weekend before Christmas, we had visitors who were delivering their own Christmas presents, and of course, we were looking forward to being taken on a long walk through the village and countryside. Then in the evening we walked to the old village church for the carol service. Imagine our surprise when we found the tower floodlit – just as if it belonged to Canterbury Cathedral or Westminster Abbey! We all thoroughly approved of this splendid idea which had evidently become established as a local custom. The bells were pealing, and as we walked up the path towards the main door we could see the silhouettes of the ringers through the tower window, looking like giant puppets on strings.

Inside the church, I was prepared for another aspect of my initiation into the life of the village. I had been invited to read one of the nine lessons from the Scriptures, which, with the carols and hymns, tell the story of the Redemption. As we had no choir to lead the singing, it is essential that the members of the congregation play their full part in the services, and they certainly did at that carol service. And it was good to hear the local schoolchildren play a couple of carols on their recorders.

In the days that followed the excitement grew, as we ticked off the list of jobs awaiting attention: icing the Christmas cake; trimming the tree and putting up the decorations; making extra beds for our guests and a thousand and one other incidentals. But in between came all the joys of the approach of Christmas: the arrival of the presents; the sound of carol singers as they made their way around the village calling in at various houses;

A village performance of *Aladdin*, 1950s.

and visits to the local pub where one heard all about other people's preparations for Christmas – as well as details of the precautions being taken to prevent snowdrifts blocking the roads.

On Christmas Eve, in accordance with our own established tradition, we downed all tools at three o'clock in the afternoon to listen to the Service of the Nine Carols and Lessons from Kings College Cambridge. How often I have wished to be in Cambridge for this particular service. But listening to it on the radio is the next best thing.

Shortly after eleven o'clock it was time to set out for the midnight service, which meant driving about four or five miles to the next village. As is often the case in rural areas, our own church is one of two served by the same priest and the midnight service was being held in the neighbouring village. It was a beautiful clear night, a typical Christmas Eve, with that magical silence which pervades over the countryside on this and the following night. All was still in the bare cornfields, which in the summer had had the appearance of a vast sea of gold. Inside the church stood a simply decorated Christmas tree, while the representation of the stable at Bethlehem was set out on the ledges of the windows in the apse behind the altar – an ingenious arrangement, obviously the result of careful thought.

And so to Christmas Day. It was the brightest and warmest Christmas I had ever known in Britain; so warm, in fact, that when we took our late morning drinks into the garden, some of our guests removed their jackets! But back to the early morning. Christmas stockings were opened, and after breakfast there was a service in our own village church. How beautiful it looked in the bright sunshine, with the flag of St George flying from the mast in the tower, while inside the floral arrangements, in honour of the Christmas festival, were the best I had ever seen. It was a well attended and largely choral service with families, normally separated for most of the year by work or school, worshipping together, and some of the younger members of the congregation jealously clutching new toys which they had seen for the first time just an hour or so before.

Back home again, the long awaited moment came when we gathered around the Christmas tree to open presents – and what a mess the room looked a short time later with discarded wrapping paper, string and gift cards strewn carelessly round. Eventually there was time for a short stroll before tackling the business of the day: the Christmas Dinner – preceded as always in our family by a glass of champagne with which we toast the health of the queen, after listening to her Christmas broadcast to the Commonwealth. The traditional midday dinner, with its several courses, is a lengthy affair, enlivened by the pulling of crackers and the distribution of small gifts from a model steam engine; and when we reach the Christmas pudding and mince pies (which we now serve with clotted cream sent direct from south-west England) it's time for reminiscing and retelling of old family stories.

In the evening we all went for a brisk walk, primarily to see the floodlit church and to enjoy the peace of the village. The weather had turned much colder, and next morning the countryside, although still bathed in bright sunshine, was white with frost.

When our guests had left, the fine weather encouraged us to spend a day or two touring the countryside by car. One of the places which we stopped at was Fairford in Gloucestershire, where, after admiring the 16th century stained glass windows in the parish church, we had afternoon tea at the Bull Hotel – served beside a roaring fire in the lounge which was still gay with Christmas decorations. We were offered hot buttered toast, I remember, with Christmas cake with blue and white icing – and then we wished we were staying on for dinner and the night. . . .

That first village Christmas of ours really came to an end on New Year's Eve. We attended a very pleasant party, and then after dinner we listened to the church bells as they rang farewell to the passing year. Later, after the stroke of midnight, the bells suddenly pealed out again over the silent countryside to give a joyful welcome to the first day of January. This was the signal for me to make my way to another house in the village, where welcome refreshments were awaiting the ringers.

# *Nativity Play*

## Iris Cannon

*I think many of us remember with a nostalgic smile the school or Sunday school nativity play, with the five-year-old pupils looking angelic in their freshly laundered, glitter-spangled pillowcase wings, and the class menace as a belligerent innkeeper shouting out his single line in staccato form: 'NO-ROOM! THERE-IS-NO-ROOM-AT-THE-INN!' Then the parade of the three kings. Mothers spent hours sewing and stitching every glass bead and fancy button in the house on to their 'jewelled' costumes. Mary pushes the donkey who is too close to her precious 'Holy Babe', and he falls off the stage midst howls of pain and indignation.*

*In the following extract, from* Housewife *magazine (1951) Ms Cannon brings back those memories as she describes a village Sunday school nativity play in the Cumberland fells.*

*The SCENE is set for the greatest of all plays; the
STAGE is a little lamplit church in the Cumberland
fells; the CAST awed but eager schoolchildren,
supported by a band of toddlers drilled to behave like
real cherubs.*

Ours is a tiny village, without even a village street or
a shop, but all who could possibly be spared from the
pressing work of farm life came along to help with
the production of our Nativity play. The father of the
principal cherub proved to be a genius in lighting
effects and, with the help of his car battery, transformed
the chancel of the church into a most effective scene,
with the Eastern star beautifully placed.

My own home was completely neglected; it took all
my time and ingenuity to contrive a costume for Gabriel,
for which angelic part our young daughter was cast.
My son, however, who had chosen, out of the Three
Kings, to be the black one, had a splendid time inventing
his own outfit, including quantities of jewellery and
burnt cork.

One point struck us all most forcibly during rehearsals,
and that was the earnestness and reverence with which
the whole cast of children regarded the learning and
acting of this wonderful old story.

Last minute emergencies cropped up, as usual, on the
day itself and, as usual, were dealt with, although it took
my son, in his rather fierce Ethiopian get-up, at least an
hour and the whole of a week's sweet ration to convince

a terrified baby cherub that he was not a dreadful stranger but an old friend in disguise.

There was a strong blizzard in force that evening, but we managed to get the children taken up to the church in cars, in detachments. The pews were well filled with friends and relations, and snug among the fells our small community gathered round the warmth of the stable to worship the Christ Child.

Many of our audience had tramped far through the blizzard to be present, and ages varied from the near eighties to the nearly one year old in arms. Some of the tinies crept into the aisle to get a better view, as the curtains were drawn apart, revealing the sweet scene of the Annunciation.

My own view of the play was rather restricted as I was in charge of the cast in the vestry, it being my duty to see that each character was ready for his or her entrance. Perhaps that made it even more real to me; the sight of the children's eager little faces as each in turn left the darkness of the vestry to go into the glare of the Chancel to bear witness for the Christ Child was an inspiration in itself.

'Where is He that is born the King of the Jews? We have seen His Star in the East, and are come to worship Him.'

As these words rang out from the West door, all heads were turned to see the Three Kings make their entrance, snow following them into the church.

Slowly and majestically they came down the aisle, while we all sang 'We Three Kings of Orient are.'

A traditional infant-school nativity play production, *Monmouthshire Beacon*.

At this point I had to leave the vestry and find my way round the outside of the church to the West door, in order to be near the Children's Corner by the font, to gather the little ones together as they came down the church in their final procession.

As I got to the door, half blinded by the snow and the darkness, a large fell sheepdog rose from the snowy step, shook himself and, with a friendly sniff, allowed me to enter – I felt his rightful place was inside the church worshipping with the rest of us.

As I entered, the Black King was just making his offering, kneeling in reverence by the Crib. In another moment the scene was over, and the cast lined up for the procession. 'Oh, come, let us adore Him' rang through the rafters in a joyful chorus as they made their way to the Children's Corner where I was waiting to gather the baby ones on to the soft warm carpet.

It was all over far too quickly and seemed no time before the children had been claimed by their mothers and grannies, bundled into waiting cars and whisked home to bed, with the sound of the Adoration of the Christ Child still ringing in their ears.

# *All Aboard for Santa's Grotto*

## Maria Hubert

'Now be good, and we will go to Lewis's this afternoon!' How many homes must have echoed with this phrase in the Yorkshire city of Leeds in the 1950s? What was so special about Lewis's? The superb Santa grotto! There were many other department stores with a similar event but for me, as for thousands of other children, it had to be Lewis's.

The queues of parents with bored yet excited children trying hard to be as good as gold stretched down all two flights of stairs and across the ground floor to the entrance, and sometimes even outside the store. Half way there would be a notice, 'One hour's wait from here'.

Seasoned queuers brought flasks, books and colouring books to keep the children occupied. Even more sensible ones went with friends and their children, so that the time might pass more quickly with the latest gossip, while the children would play together.

Once on the second floor, parents would sidle off, leaving their children with the next parent in line for a short while, while they got some secret shopping from the toy department or maybe a quick cuppa from the cafeteria, also conveniently placed on the second floor.

For a child of five it was sheer magic. This huge space filled top to bottom with toys of every conceivable type. Dolls and wonderfully 'grown-up' prams stood against displays with nodding snowmen and digging elves. Somewhere, someone was singing all the popular Christmas songs. Everything sparkled! And just ahead was the magical mysterious archway to the ride of a lifetime.

One year it was a huge sleigh, which bumped and rolled over the snowy scene while a moving screen showed the scenery passing by. Another year it was Santa's express train, rushing along an alpine pass. The last one I remember was a spaceship to the moon! Inside the ship, with its silvery curved sides, I could sit by a porthole window and watch as stars and comets passed us by, and the occasional elf on its way to earth to check on good children.

We always entered the vehicle from a door in the rear, and filed out througha door in front. This door held

Refreshments for Santa, anonymous illustration, 1923.

more magic for us all, as we held our breath in anticipation of what lay beyond. It could be Santa's Mines, with Snow White's dwarfs digging away in caverns sparkling with gemstones, a snowy landscape with several animated scenes of elven activity, more nodding snowmen and reindeer. One year all the woodland folk seemed to be going in the same direction we were, pointing and waving. The last scene was the stable at Bethlehem, complete with (again nodding) ox and ass and sound effects.

But always at the end was the grotto. Lush with sparkling cottonwool snow, sitting on a huge throne,

Santa's grotto, 1940s.

with an entourage of fairies and elves – there would be
Father Christmas and his special 'Good Fairy' with the
prettiest dress of pink and white who was there to help
the shy children overcome their awe. It was breathtaking.
Some of the more timid children would hold back at
first, but with a little encouragement from the Good
Fairy, we all found ourselves chatting to Father
Christmas about our hearts' desires as if we were old
friends – which of course, as good little children – we
were! Children usually asked for one or two presents and
maybe a couple of small gifts as well. A dolly and pram;

a desk and blackboard; a clockwork train set, never wanting to seem greedy by asking for too much. When pressed, some children would ask for a dolly's tea set, a 'Rupert' annual, a football or a cowboy outfit as well.

All too soon it was time to say goodbye, and Father Christmas would give us a toy from one of his sacks – left sack for girls, right sack for boys. Sometimes he had a third smaller sack that the Good Fairy looked after, which held presents for older boys and girls. It was not unusual in the early 1950s to see children of ten and eleven going to visit Father Christmas.

Back we would go, clutching magical painting books (my favourite), colouring books and crayons, paper cap guns, Indian feather head-dresses, small dolls and motorcars, which we thought were wonderful, for had they not come from Father Christmas himself? The ride back ended quickly, and we were trooped out of the back door again. Some of the older children usually asked why, and it was always the same sort of reply, the other end had landed in a snow-drift, or the door was jammed! Then we would be taken for tea as most children, the excitement over, were hungry, having been too agitated to eat lunch. For me it was always Young's Fish Restaurant for a fish and chip supper with brown bread and butter and tea. Such happy memories, yet how many ten-year-olds today would quietly accept all the magical hype? It is considered 'uncool' – but it was also great fun!

# 'A Christmas Epilogue'

## William Makepeace Thackeray

*This epilogue is as fitting an end for this small book as it was when it was written 150 years ago as the conclusion to one of Thackeray's acclaimed Christmas books, which were published each year. This epilogue follows the tale of an assistant headmaster at an academy of learning in the fictitious town of Rodwell Regis.*

The play is done; the curtain drops,
Slow falling, to the prompter's bell
A moment yet the actor stops,
And looks around, to say farewell.
It is an irksome word and task;
And when he's laughed and said his say,
He shows, as he removes the mask,
A face that's anything but gay.
One word, ere yet the evening ends,
Let's close it with a parting rhyme,
And pledge a hand to all young friends,
As fits the merry Christmas-time.
On life's wide scene you, too, have parts,
That Fate ere long shall bid you play;
Good night! with honest gentle hearts
A kindly greeting go alway!
A gentleman, or old or young
(Bear kindly with my humble lays):

Angels appear to the shepherds, Vizelly Brothers, 1840.

The sacred chorus first was sung
Upon the first of Christmas days.
The shepherds heard it overhead
The joyful angels raised it then:
Glory to heaven on high, it said,
And peace on earth to gentle men.

My song, save this, is little worth
I lay the weary pen aside,
And wish you health, and love, and mirth,
As fits the solemn Christmas tide.
As fits the holy Christmas birth,
Be this, good friends, our carol still
Be peace on earth, be peace on earth,
To men of gentle will.

# Sources and Bibliography

Acton, R., 'The First Wassail', from the *Illustrated London News*, Christmas 1871

Bonham, Mrs John, 'Cornish Cakes and Customs', from *Christmas in Cornwall Sixty Years Ago*, Unicorn Press, 1898

'Candied Walnuts, English Caramels and Preserved Violets', from *Home Notes*, 1898

Cannon, Iris, 'Nativity Play', from *Housewife* magazine, 1951

*The Diary of Samuel Pepys*, Bell & Sons, 1926

Duffin, Ruth and Celia, 'Christmas Eve', from *Escape*, Dent, 1920

Griffiths, Glyn, 'The Wondrous Tree of Christmas', from *Country Quest Christmas Book*, 1964; with grateful thanks to the editor for permission to use this story

Horne, Richard Henry, *The Memoirs of a London Doll*, Joseph Cundall, 1846

*John Evelyn's Memoirs*, 1818; some diary entries are taken from the *Tatler*, 1951

Kipling, Rudyard, 'A Fenland Carol' and 'Eddi's Service', from *Rewards and Fairies*, 1910

*Memoirs of Thomas Bewick*, ed. John Lane, The Bodley Head, 1924

Palmer, Cyril, 'Village Christmas', from the *Tatler* magazine, 1951

*Paupers and Pig Killers, The Diary of William Holland, A Somerset Parson, 1799–1818*, ed. J. Ayres, Gloucester, Sutton Publishing, 1984

'The Royal Christmases of Queen Victoria', reproduced by kind permission of her gracious Majesty, Queen Elizabeth II and also by kind permission of the *Tatler* magazine, Christmas 1955

'The Second Shepherd's Play', from *The Wakefield Mysteries*, 1917 (private publication)

Thackeray, William Makepeace, 'A Christmas Epilogue', from *Doctor Birch*, Chapman & Hall, 1849

Thackeray, William Makepeace, 'Being an Essay on Thunder and Small Beer', from *History of the Kickleburys Abroad*, Smith, Elder & Co., 2nd edn, 1850

The short extract from the Duchess of Hamilton's papers is taken from an unidentified page.

Bringing in the yule-log, late nineteenth-century Christmas card.

# Acknowledgements

I am grateful to the many publishers, editors and authors who have given permission for their work to be used, and to a few who are no longer around or cannot be traced. I hope that you will take the inclusion of your work as the compliment intended. I particularly thank the publishers of the works listed in the bibliography for permission to reproduce them or extracts from them.

Original research, translations and presentation of historical facts are by Maria Hubert. All unacknowledged material is taken from the Christmas Archives Research Library. All illustrations are reproduced courtesy of the Christmas Archives Picture Library.

The original artwork for 'Christmas Eve' and 'Eddi's Christmas' are courtesy of Jung-Sook Nam Hubert.

I especially acknowledge the former Tom Smith Cracker Company, Norwich (particularly the late Mr Varney), for the story about the origins of the Christmas cracker. I also thank my husband Andrew for all his work with the scanner and computer. And to everyone who has helped me on this series of books – family, friends, strangers who became friends, editorial staff at Sutton Publishing, artists and authors who permitted use of their work, and the many librarians and archivists – my most grateful thanks.